* * * * * *

The
New
You

* * * * * *

The New You

* * * * * *

by Dede Robertson

THOMAS NELSON PUBLISHERS
NASHVILLE • CAMDEN • NEW YORK

Published in Nashville, Tennessee, by Thomas Nelson, Inc. and distributed in Canada by Lawson Falle, Ltd., Cambridge, Ontario.

Printed in the United States of America.

Unless otherwise noted, Scripture quotations are from THE NEW KING JAMES VERSION. Copyright © 1979, 1980, 1982, Thomas Nelson, Inc., Publishers.

Scripture quotations noted TEV are from the *Good News Bible*—Old Testament: Copyright © American Bible Society 1976; New Testament: Copyright © American Bible Society 1966, 1971, 1976. Used by permission.

Scripture quotations noted RSV are from the Revised Standard Version of the Bible, copyrighted © 1946, 1952, © 1971, 1973.

ISBN 0-8407-5408-6

Contents

CHAPTER ONE # We Have a Weight Problem

I have a weight problem. In fact, almost everyone I know has a weight problem.

It may be a matter of five pounds, ten pounds, twenty pounds, or much, much more. But whatever the amount, most people are concerned about any extra fat—and the unsightliness that accompanies every ballooning waistline, hip bulge, flabby arm, or too-ample derriere.

As a general rule, the older we get, the more difficult it is to maintain a proper weight. For many, the source of the excess poundage may be a change in bodily metabolism, or perhaps it's a more sedentary way of living that we settle into as the years pass. For others, the married state may even be related to their weight woes.

Yes, marriage. A 1983 survey of *Weight Watchers* magazine readers revealed that the degree of connubial bliss was a key factor in weight gain: Although people typically add pounds as the years go by anyway, the average unhappy wife was *fifty-four pounds* overweight, while happily married wives were "only" twenty-four pounds above their optimum weight.

Whether you're married or single, the usual solution to the poundage problem is some "miracle" diet—a panacea that weight-loss clinics and book publishers promise will eliminate forever all excess flab. Unfortunately, too many of the highly touted formulas don't work at all; or if they do work, it's only for a short time.

Even if you manage to take off those extra inches and firm up your sagging sections, before long you find yourself putting the pounds right back on. What diet experts call the "yo-yo syndrome" goes into effect. That is, the pounds go down, but then they inevitably come right back. You may begin to wonder if there's something in the "nature of the universe" that causes your body to return to the overweight level where you were before you even thought about a diet program.

Actually, there may be something very basic in our physical makeup that causes our weight to move back up after we've struggled successfully to take it off. You see, many individuals overeat in response to stress. First of all, we get frustrated, anxious, or depressed; then, almost immediately—to inject a little pleasure and happiness back into our lives—we turn to the refrigerator.

At the root of this normal, often unconscious emotional grasping for food, there may be a chemical drive that impels us to stuff ourselves. Recently, scientists have discovered that people who eat when the pressures of life get too burdensome may be responding to natural, stress-induced opiates that the body produces in times of pressure. Among other things, these bodily chemicals make us hungry. Unless we possess significant resources in our lives that counter stress and give us inner peace, the drive to eat in the wake of pressure may become overwhelming.

The Consequences of Being Overweight

What happens when you are overweight and out of shape? Here are some of the adverse consequences:

1. *Your energy levels decline markedly.* Generally speaking, people who carry extra weight on their bodies or who avoid exercise like the plague lack staying power in the midst of life's daily demands. Even if they can operate at high energy levels for a while during the day, they tend to run out of steam before the afternoon is over. If you're obese or sedentary, you may make it through part or most of a workday or workweek only to find that you have nothing left for your family, hobbies, or recreational or service activities outside the home.

2. *Your health may go into a tailspin.* Dr. Kenneth Cooper, founder of the Aerobics Center in Dallas and a world-renowned expert on exercise and diet, has found that obesity and sedentary living are two of the major factors that accompany heart disease and other physical ailments.

In his *Aerobics Program for Total Well-Being*, Dr. Cooper says,

Carrying just five extra pounds around the middle or on the bottom may create a deadlier drag on the body than most people, including many physicians, now imagine. We already know definitely that being *grossly* over-weight—say 30 or 40 pounds or more—can contribute to all sorts of life-threatening health problems, like coronary disease and cancer. But it may also well be that *any* amount of extra fat in some way acts as a trigger for much more serious diseases (p. 67).

If you stay fat and inactive, you may not reap the whirlwind of sickness and incapacity this year or the next. But you do have an appointment with serious problems somewhere down the road. And probably, you'll find yourself confronting those problems much earlier than if you begin now to take care of the body God has entrusted to you.

3. *Your sense of self-confidence will suffer.* Pride in your appearance can degenerate into vanity. But failure to keep yourself as trim and attractive as possible can aggravate any insecurities and uncertainties you may feel about yourself.

To illustrate this, let me suggest you try an experiment: Go into a department store wearing the oldest, dirtiest, most ragged clothes you own and see how the sales force responds to you. Then, a few days later, go into that same store in a smart, well-tailored outfit. I've done this, and if you try it, I imagine you'll find what I did: When I looked slovenly, I was treated like a slovenly person, and in response I actually felt bad about myself. When I looked sharp, I was treated with great deference, and my self-confidence was buoyed.

By the same token, if you're out of shape, overweight, and run down, people will respond to you more negatively than if you appear trim, vigorous, and energetic. If you suffer at all from any lack of self-confidence, you can bet those feelings of inferiority will worsen when you detect those negative responses to your physical appearance.

A vicious cycle can be the result: Your self-confidence is low, so you turn to the refrigerator for comfort. You overeat and gain more weight, and your self-confidence sinks even lower. So you turn to food again...

For the Christian, such issues are very important, because it is with these bodies that we serve the Lord. If they are overweight and out of shape, if we lack energy and self-esteem because of our physical condition, we will not be as effective in His service as we could and should be.

I believe each of us has a certain divinely ordained, highly individual physical potential. Further, I am convinced that God wants us to reach that potential so that we can be as effective as possible in working for Him.

Of course, this does not mean it is necessary to become an Olympic athlete to reach your full physical or spiritual potential. Clearly, if that were the requirement, few of us would make it—least of all me. Each of us has a *unique* potential. There are many outstanding saints, for example, who have lost significant physical powers because of disease, accident, or age. But there are also many fine Christians who might be very surprised at how much more efficiently they could live and work if they developed their bodies to their full, God-given potential.

There is an even better reason, however, for getting and staying in shape. I refer to the incredible truth about Christians declared by the apostle Paul in 1 Corinthians 6:19-20: "Do you not know that your body is the temple of the Holy Spirit who is in you, whom you have from God, and you are not your own? For you were bought at a price; therefore glorify God in your body and in your spirit, which are God's."

Those are amazing statements, aren't they? God is actually living in the Christian's body, which He has called His "temple." When we realize that this is one of the reasons for which the human body was made, we can understand that we all have a tremendous responsibility for the proper care of our bodies.

At this point, you may be saying to yourself, "All right, I can agree on the need to get and keep my weight under control. What will this book do for me to help me achieve that?" The answer to that question is in the pages that follow, and you may find this book will do a great deal more for you than you had anticipated if you picked it up expecting only another diet book. You may well find that weight loss will be only the first step toward the discovery of a whole New You.

CHAPTER TWO # Weight Loss Is Only the Beginning

Y our main goal in picking up this book was to learn how to lose weight. Losing weight was a concern of mine, too, and I tried just about every fad diet that came along. I experienced that yo-yo syndrome we talked about earlier, losing weight but putting it back on just a short time later. It looked as though I would never achieve permanent weight loss. However, my weight is now under control, and the way I gained that control is what I am going to show you in this book.

Let me emphasize, though, that there is another dimension to the New You idea, which is the really exciting part of the program. You see, the key I found to permanent weight control opens the door to a whole New You—happier, healthier, more fulfilled—*in every area of life*. That key is in one sense very simple; yet its effects can be life-changing.

What I learned is that on my own it is nearly impossible to maintain the motivation and self-discipline essential to achieving anything worthwhile. Self-discipline, I know, sounds negative, but it is really the passport to freedom. The undisciplined person is the one who never achieves his or her goals and has trouble accomplishing the things he or she wants and needs to do.

This is typical, isn't it? Whether we want to become skilled pianists, public speakers, tennis players, or gourmet cooks—or whether we want to lose and keep off extra pounds—we tend to start off like balls of fire. But in the long stretches, we find our inner resources aren't enough. They let us down because we lack firm cores of self-discipline.

The solution to this problem is to draw upon the spiritual re-

11

sources offered by God through the indwelling Holy Spirit. That sounds simple, but it's not. In my life, it meant as never before that I had to turn consciously to God in studying the Bible, in prayer, and in meditation. It meant allowing God to change me in all areas of my life and allowing Him to do that gradually—not expecting overnight total transformation. Unless I had learned to draw consistently on God's strength and resources in this area, I never would have been able to gain control of my weight.

When I began to apply spiritual principles to my weight control efforts, I saw that I had the possibility of a whole new lifestyle. I could become not just a new me physically but also a new me spiritually, emotionally, mentally, socially—in all areas of my life.

The reason is that we are whole people. What we are like in one area of life is essentially what we are like in all the other areas as well. Basic changes in one area, therefore, are also going to affect each of the other areas.

Let me illustrate this by looking at the crucial matter of self-discipline. If you have not yet acquired the necessary motivation and discipline in the area of eating and exercise, chances are you aren't properly motivated and self-disciplined in other areas either. Some people can be very disciplined in one area of their lives and undisciplined in others, and we all do at least a little better in some things than in others. But generally speaking, we fall pretty much into one of two camps. We are either motivated, self-disciplined people (the minority), or we are not (the majority).

If we have acquired the motivation to get things done and have learned to discipline ourselves accordingly, we tend to be effective in every area of our lives. We get the job done, well and on time, in the office and at home. In the spiritual realm, we recognize the importance of prayer, Bible study, fellowship, and Christian work, and we make time for these things regularly and often. We routinely devote time and effort to helping, teaching, and enjoying our children, and to helping and enjoying our spouses and friends. Simply put, a self-disciplined person is a disciplined person in all areas of life.

On the other hand, just the opposite is true of people who are generally undisciplined. I am guessing with some confidence that most of you who have been losing the struggle with weight control are also not as disciplined as you'd like to be in other areas of your lives. You don't get as much done as you'd like. If you kept careful track for a few days, you'd probably find you're wasting a lot of time. You may have a habit of being late for work, church, and meetings. If you're Christian, chances are you don't pray and study the Bible the way you know you should.

Your basic habits and approaches to doing things are consistent throughout the spectrum of your life. Thus, if you apply spiritual principles and draw on God's resources in the area of your physical condition and thereby start to gain control over your weight, you will also be in a position to do the same thing in the other parts of your life. Let's see, in practical terms, how these comprehensive interchanges can occur—and eventually produce the New You.

The New, Improved You

The largest part of this book is devoted to a ten-week diet schedule. For each day you will find a complete menu for all three meals, plus a snack. You will also find a devotional and a suggested prayer for each day. These are crucial to the weight control program because they will train you to draw on God's strength and they will teach you the specific spiritual principles you need to apply.

Consider now what this could also mean to your spiritual life. Have you unsuccessfully struggled to start or maintain a daily devotional life, even though you know it is the key to fellowship with and growth in the Lord? In this program, you will have a devotional time for seventy consecutive days. That's a good start on a new and spiritually fruitful habit, isn't it?

Also, think what this can mean in your emotional life. As you spend time with God and learn to draw upon His resources to get control of your life, will it not become much easier to find His strength to help you through your times of fear, depression, loneliness, and other emotional trials?

Yes, becoming a New You physically opens the way for an entire New You. What we are talking about is the full truth of 2 Corinthians 5:17: "Therefore, if anyone is in Christ, he is a new creation; old things have passed away; behold, all things have become new." A Christian becomes a new creation spiritually at the moment he or she places trust for salvation in Jesus Christ, and that is the primary meaning of this verse. But it is also possible, through the power of the indwelling Holy Spirit, to become a new creation in every area of our daily lives, and that is God's earnest desire for us.

Three cautions need to be sounded at this point. First, if you are not a Christian, a believer in and follower of Jesus Christ, the spiritual resources of which I have been speaking will elude you. It also means the devotional portion of the ten-week diet program that follows will make little sense. Anyone can use the diet menus and exercises given in this book, but the spiritual principles that are the cornerstone of this program are essential to long-term success.

Second, you should consult your physician before embarking on any diet or exercise program.

Third, you need to keep in mind that the key to permanent success in weight control is to lose excess pounds at a steady, persistent, relatively slow pace. Many fad diets try to give you rapid and large weight losses, but often this lost weight is water. These are the kinds of programs that lead to the yo-yo syndrome. Proper weight loss needs to be gradual but steady. As you diet, you must continue to eat nutritionally complete and balanced meals. You must also learn new habits of eating and exercise, and that takes time.

Similarly, in other areas of life, old habits die hard. Remember that as with proper weight loss you are looking for steady, sure progress. If certain habits or areas of your life seem to remain out of control after a period of time don't despair. As you depend upon God and draw upon His resources, the motivation and self-discipline will come. As Philippians 2:13 tells us, "It is God who works in you both to will and to do for His good pleasure."

CHAPTER THREE **How to Stretch and Strengthen the Body and Spirit**

ome people feel the most beautiful sight in the world is a blazing orange sunset, set like a celestial jewel against some stunning natural background. Others may point to a magnificent work of art. But as for me, I think there's nothing more wondrous and satisfying to the eye than a healthy human body in motion.

Our bodies were created for action, not for stagnation. Plants may flourish even though they stay rooted to one spot, and some slow-moving animals, like the lowly snail, do just fine as they inch along over a quite limited patch of terrain. But people are designed to move about more vigorously during the day.

Yes, there are times when it's important to be still, times to rest, times to slow down the breakneck pace of our lives. Too often, it's not physical exercise, but a flurry of lightning-fast mental activity that makes many of us feel tired and causes us to want to rest.

Others may engage in athletics or calisthenics only sporadically—perhaps just on weekends. Such irregular, strenuous activity may well do more harm than good. Our physical systems, especially the heart, must be conditioned through regular exercise to withstand the pressures of sudden, violent movement. Consequently, most exercise experts and preventive medicine specialists strongly advocate some sort of regular, "aerobic" exercise, which is just another term for a steady, endurance-oriented workout. This type of activity, which is to be performed at least three times a week, should cause the heart rate to rise to about two-thirds of its maximum rate for a period of twenty to thirty consecutive minutes.

At the same time, there is another important reason for regular exercise, one that is directly related to weight loss. Specifically, Dr. Martin Katahn, author of *The 200 Calorie Solution*, and others recommend combining exercise with a reasonable calorie intake to achieve longer-lasting weight loss.

Here's the reason: It seems that if you cut down on your calories *without* exercising, the body just adjusts its metabolic rate downward and your ability to lose weight decreases. In other words, even if you cut your calories way down—below eight hundred a day—the rate at which you burn calories also tends to go down. That means that you lose less weight than you expected with such a low food intake. When you go off the diet, you tend to gain weight much faster than you ever did in the past, even though you may be eating less food than you did before you started the diet.

On the other hand, by combining exercise with a somewhat lower but still reasonable calorie intake, you can keep your metabolism up and burn more calories during your dieting program. Also, you'll find that it will be easier to *keep* the weight off, especially if you continue with your higher rate of physical activity.

In the New You diet, exercise plays an important role for all these reasons. I believe that the human body has been put together in such a way that it *demands* regular exercise in order to function well. It's clear to me from the latest medical evidence, as well as from my own experience, that exercise is an essential ingredient in any complete, long-term weight loss program.

Over the years, I have formulated my own exercise program to complement my weight-reduction and weight-maintenance efforts. I began doing exercises regularly when I was in college. Gradually, I added extra activities and fine-tuned old ones until now I have fifteen basic exercises that I do about four times a week. Also, I combine them with a vigorous one- to two-mile walk and some tennis several times a week. This program provides the basis for my personal physical shape-up program that I'm about to share with you.

These exercises, like the diet program we'll discuss in the next section, aren't designed to be performed in a vacuum. As I mentioned in the previous chapter, I believe the only way you can increase your chances of taking weight off and keeping it off is to create a "New You." In other words, you need to develop an "inner person" who is highly motivated to stay in shape because her weight-maintenance program has been thoroughly integrated with her personal philosophy of life.

As far as exercise is concerned, this means that I always try to do my fifteen activities just after I have my morning devotionals. I'll first spend some time in prayer and Bible reading. Then, with this "spiritual momentum" moving me along, I'll continue to pray and meditate, even as I embark on my exercise program.

I suggest you begin to use the daily diet-and-devotional guide outlined in the next section. Begin with the Bible reading, the meditation, and the short prayer. Then, with your mind focused on God and on how He wants to enter into your approach to food and physical exercise, you can begin with the fifteen-step workout. You may want to top the exercises off, as I often do, with a short walk, jog, or swim. Finally, as you follow the twelve hundred calorie weight-loss menus during the rest of the day, you'll most likely find the spiritual momentum you began with your devotionals and continued with your exercises will greatly increase your will power and motivation when you finally dig into your food.

This, in a nutshell, is what *The New You* diet and exercise program is all about. Now, let's get started with the exercises.

The following exercises are designed to be performed over a period of fifteen to thirty minutes, depending on the number of repetitions of each that you do. To get the full aerobic effect of these exercises—that is, to get your heart rate up to a high enough level to condition your heart and cardiovascular system—it's important to maintain a steady series of movements, with no rests between exercises. You may find you have to rest when you first start this program. Your goal should be to move immediately from one activity to the next until all fifteen have been completed.

No. 1: The Super Stretch

To start your exercises on an upbeat note, it's helpful to choose a word or two from the Bible or a short prayer, such as "Rejoice!" or "Peace and joy!" Then, repeat that phrase silently to yourself during this warm-up exercise. Your words could be taken from the biblical passage you've read the first thing in the morning or from one of the devotional readings in the next chapter.

1.   Lie flat on your back, with arms extended on the floor above your head. Your legs should be flat on the floor and fairly close together.

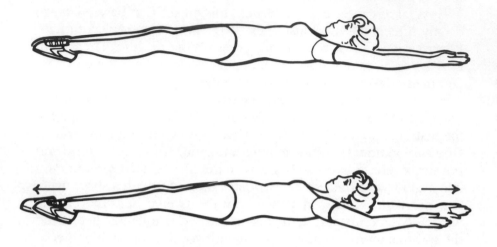

2.   Rotate your right hand so that your palm is facing upward, away from your head. *Note*: Since you're lying flat on your back for this exercise, the terms "upward" and "downward" don't refer to the directions toward the ceiling or floor, but rather the directions away from your body, as though you were standing up straight.

3.   Push the heel of your right hand and the rest of your right arm upward, away from your head, and at the same time push your right heel and leg downward. You should feel a stretching tension along the entire right side of your body as you make these moves. Your neck and elbows should remain as relaxed as possible during this activity, however.

4.   Execute four distinct stretches on the right side in steady but fairly quick succession, following a "1-2-3-4" rhythm.

5.   Repeat these movements on the left side of your body.

6.   Do the exercises six times on each side, and work up to ten over a period of four weeks.

No. 2: The Palm-to-Knee Pumper

In this movement, designed to firm up the waist and upper back, try thinking of things you should praise God for in your life.

1.   Lie flat on your back, with your arms at your sides, palms

turned toward the ceiling. Your legs should be spread out comfortably, straight on the floor.

2.   Raise your left leg up at a 45-degree angle to the floor, with your left knee slightly bent.

3.   Immediately move your right hand, palm still turned toward the ceiling, over to touch the left knee. Your shoulders should remain flat on the floor during this movement. The entire movement should be executed in a "1-2-3" rhythm, with your left leg first coming up, then your right hand touching your left knee, and finally the return of your leg and arm to the floor in the starting position.

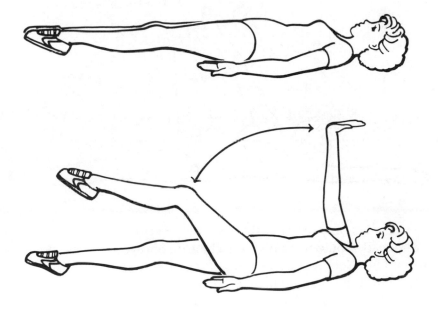

4.   Repeat with the right leg and left arm.

5.   Begin with ten repetitions for each side, and work up to twenty.

No. 3: The Side-Splitting Stretch

As you do this stretching exercise for the waist and upper hips, you might focus on ways that God wants you to "stretch yourself" spiritually, or grow closer to His likeness.

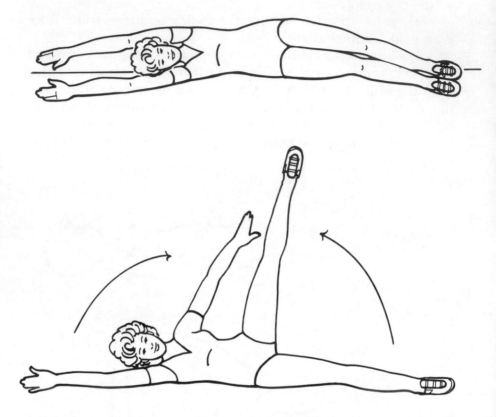

1.   Lie on your right side, with your arms stretched overhead. Your head should rest on your right arm, and your palms should be turned up. Keep your legs straight, but bend your body around to the right in a slight semicircle on the floor.

2.   Raise your left leg toward the ceiling, and simultaneously raise your left arm so that you touch your left leg with your left hand.

3.   Return your arm and leg to the floor and resume the semicircular position, so that your left arm and leg are now once again extended in a stretch.

4.   Begin with eight repetitions and then turn to the other side and repeat. Work up to fifteen on each side over a period of four weeks.

No. 4: The Pendulum Swing

This rolling technique, where your body moves back and forth on the floor like a pendulum, will shape the hips, waist, and abdomen. As your lower body swings back and forth, it's natural to focus on how many things in life are unstable and uncertain yet become manageable when Christ provides a stable center.

1.   Begin by lying on your back, with arms extended out to your sides. Your palms should be turned up to the ceiling, and your knees bent up against your chest, with your feet off the floor.

2.   Keeping your knees together, roll your legs over to the right side just off the floor.

3.   Move your knees upward until they are about even with your extended right arm.

4.   Roll your legs back to the original position, and repeat the exercise on the left side.

5.   Do ten repetitions on each side, and try to work up to twenty-five repetitions within four to six weeks.

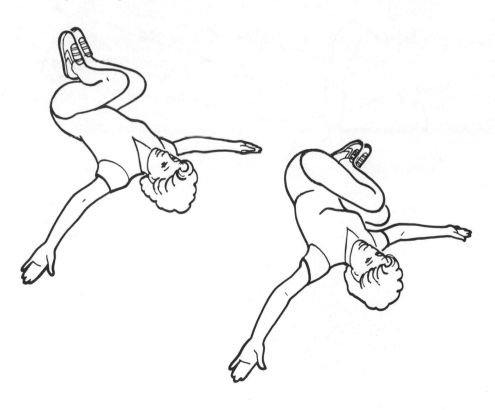

No. 5: The Side-Bike Racer

This excellent exercise for the thighs, knees, and calves involves bicycling movements. As you do these movements, it may be helpful to think of Paul's admonition to "finish the race" of spiritual growth and mission (see 2 Tim. 4:7).

1.   Lie on your right side in a slight semicircle.

2.   Raise the upper part of your body on your right elbow and your left hand, and simultaneously lift both your legs slightly off the floor.

3.   Begin to execute a peddling motion with your legs.

4.   Count one cycle each time your left leg is extended and continue up to a count of eighteen. Then switch to the other side and perform an equal number of repetitions. Over a four- to six-week period, work up to thirty repetitions on each side.

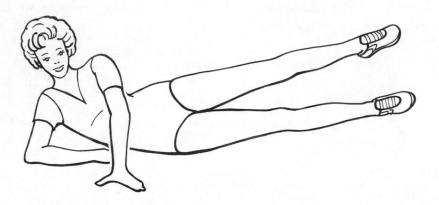

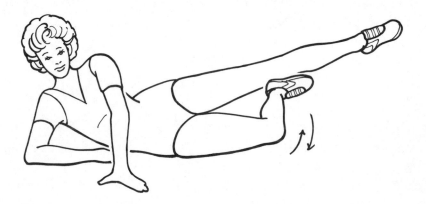

No. 6: The New You Crossover

This leg crossover, to condition the waist and hips, can help you focus on how *you* can "cross over," from the old you to the New You.

1. Lie on your back, with your arms extended out to the sides, palms turned toward the ceiling and shoulders level and flat on the floor.

2. Raise your left leg off the floor, with your left knee slightly bent and pointing toward the ceiling.

3. Cross your left leg over your body, and touch the floor near your right hand with your left foot.

4. Bring your left leg back across your body and return it slowly to the starting position on the floor.

5. Repeat this motion with your right leg.

6. Begin by performing eight repetitions with each leg, and work up to twenty repetitions over a four-week period.

No. 7: The Backbone Lift

Any system designed to further physical or spiritual development requires "backbone," or a tough, resilient commitment to stick with the program through thick and thin. As you do this exercise, which will help you strengthen your trunk muscles and straighten your shoulders and spine, you might regard it as symbolic of the firm personal commitment you've made with the New You diet.

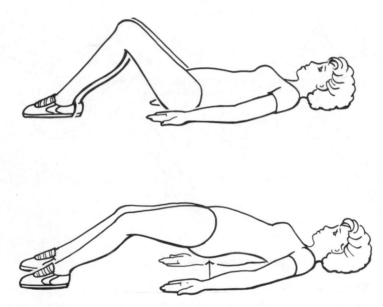

1.   Lie on your back with your arms on the floor, at a 45-degree angle from your body. Your palms should be turned up toward the ceiling, your knees bent at a 45-degree angle, and your feet together, flat on the floor.

2.   Raise your spine slowly off the floor, beginning at the tailbone. Lift up your trunk until your entire body is raised and resting on your shoulders, head, and feet. Your neck should be firmly pressed against the floor, but try to keep your chin up.

3.   Slowly return your spine to the floor, beginning at the neck and going down to your tailbone.

4.   Repeat this movement three times at first, and over a three to four-week period, work up to five repetitions.

No. 8: Kick Up Your Heels

This vigorous abdomen exercise is a good reminder that a regular exercise program can give us added energy to "kick up our heels" even if we may feel we're getting too old for such antics. Also, these movements are symbolic of the fact that we should kick bad health habits away so that we have the best chance to develop good habits, like proper eating and exercising.

1. Lie on your back, with your arms extended at right angles to your body. Keep your shoulders level on the floor, with your waist down against the floor and your palms turned up toward the ceiling. Your knees should be bent at a 45-degree angle, with your feet together, flat on the floor.

2. With your waist and shoulders remaining firmly pressed against the floor, bring your right knee up to your chest. Then straighten your entire right leg toward the ceiling in a slow-motion kick.

3. Slowly lower your extended right leg to the floor.

4. Extend your bent left leg down flat on the floor next to your right leg.

5. Slowly raise both legs a few inches off the floor.

6. Lower both legs flat against the floor, and then in the same motion bend both of them back to the starting position, with both feet flat on the floor and knees bent at a 45-degree angle.

7. Repeat this motion with the left leg.

8. Do four repetitions with each leg, and over a three to four-week period, work up to six repetitions.

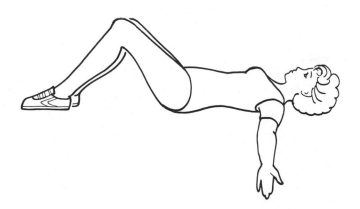

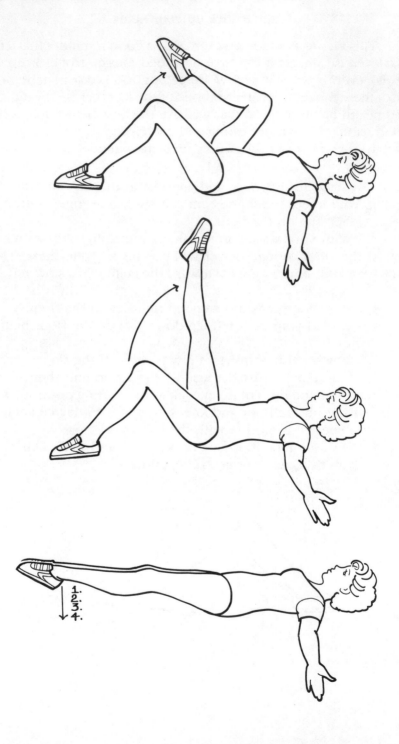

No. 9: The Good News Bicycle

The apostle Paul, quoting the prophet Isaiah, said, "How beautiful are the feet of those who preach the gospel of peace" (Rom. 10:15). When I'm watching my feet churning around in this bicycling exercise, I sometimes think how important it is to use them for a purpose—and especially to take the message of the gospel to those who haven't heard it.

1.   Lie on the floor with your arms extended out to your sides at a 70-degree angle and insert a small pillow underneath your hips. Pull your knees up toward your chest, so that your feet are suspended off the floor.

2.   Rotate your legs and feet in a stationary bicycling movement.

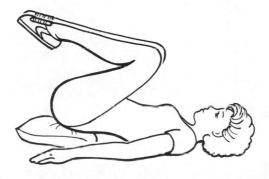

3.   Count one repetition every time your right leg returns to a tucked position in front of you. Begin with sixteen full repetitions, and over a four- to six-week period, try to work up to fifty to sixty repetitions.

No. 10: Circles in the Air

This circular thigh exercise is great for firming up the upper thighs and abdomen.

1.   Lie on your back, with your arms extended at right angles from your body. Your palms should be turned up toward the ceiling, and your shoulders and waist should stay firmly pressed against the floor.

2.   Bring your left knee up, and plant your left foot flat on the floor, as close to your hips as you can get it.

3.   Raise your **right leg** straight up toward the ceiling, and keep your right knee straight.

4.   Finally, begin to rotate your right leg in sweeping circles, as though you're tracing circles in the air with your feet.

5.   Repeat with your left leg.

6.   Repeat again with your right leg, but this time reverse the direction of the circle.

7.   Repeat with your left leg, with the circle once again reversed.

8.   Begin with eight circles in each direction with each leg, and work up to fifteen over a four- to six-week period.

No. 11: Sit Up and Stretch

Sit-ups are one of the best exercises a person can do to strengthen the waist and abdomen, and this strengthening of the trunk also helps prevent back problems.

1.   Lie on your back, with your arms extended on the floor behind you, above your head, and your palms turned toward the ceiling. Your legs should be bent at the knees and spread apart.

(*Note*: Medical experts emphasize that it's important to keep the legs bent because that puts less stress on your back and reduces the risk of a back injury.)

2.   In a steady, continuous motion, sit up and simultaneously bring your hands forward and try to touch your left foot. At first, you may not be able to get all the way down to your foot, but after a few weeks, you'll find yourself getting much more limber.

3.   Next, shift your body to the right so that you are leaning forward with both hands on the floor between your legs.

4.   Slowly lean back and lower yourself to the starting position.

5.   Reverse these movements by sitting up and reaching your hands toward your right foot.

6.   Repeat the entire cycle four times, and after about three to four weeks, work up to ten repetitions.

No. 12: Hip Walk and Roll

At first glance, this "hip walking and rolling" exercise may seem awkward and perhaps too difficult to try. But let me urge you to "walk by faith" with these unusual movements, and they'll eventually pay off with a firm trunk and a trimmer set of hips.

1.   Sit on the floor with your legs slightly spread and stretched straight out in front of you. Your hands should be resting comfortably on your knees.

2.   Now, begin to "walk" forward on your hips by shifting your weight first to the right hip and then to the left. Take ten of these hip-steps, and try to make as much forward progress as you can as you shift your weight back and forth.

3.   Next, for the "hip roll" segment, sit up straight and keep your legs straight out in front of you, flat on the floor, with your arms extended down to the floor on each side of your hips.

4.   Shift your weight to the right by rolling over on your right hip and supporting your weight on your right hand. Simultaneously, raise your left arm up over your head.

5.   Then, roll in the opposite direction by reversing this movement.

6.   Execute four rolls on each side.

7.   Finally, "walk" backward ten "steps" on your hips, and then perform four more rolls on each side of your body.

8.   You should begin by doing two complete sequences of

this "hip walk and roll." Over a four-week period, work up to ten complete sequences.

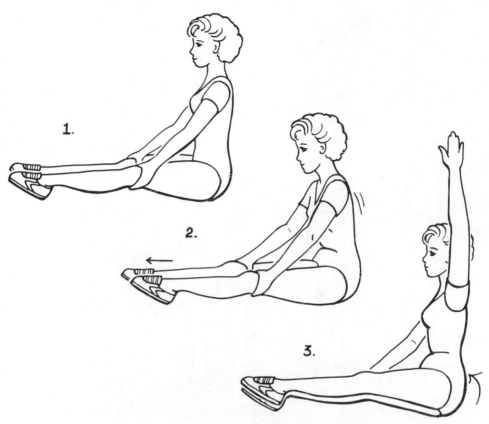

NO. 13: The Eagle Stretch

One of my favorite passages in the Old Testament is Isaiah 40:31: "Those who wait on the LORD/Shall renew their strength;/ They shall mount up with wings like eagles,/They shall run and not be weary,/They shall walk and not faint." This three-part stretching exercise is for the waist, hips, and back, and the expansive arm and body motions remind me of the great spiritual and physical endurance God can give us if we just "wait" for Him and seek His will.

Part I:

1. Stand with your feet slightly apart and both arms extended overhead.

2. Stretch both arms upward, as though you were trying to fly up toward heaven to praise God.

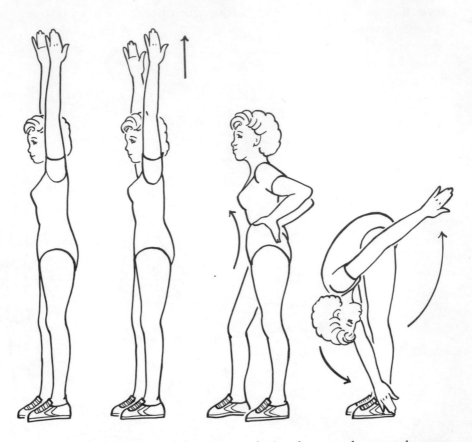

3. Relax your right arm and simultaneously stretch your left arm upward.

4. Relax your left arm and simultaneously stretch your right arm upward. Repeat this motion six times with each arm.

Part II:

5. Spread your legs farther apart and place your hands on your hips.

6. Bend to the right three times rather quickly, but without excessively jerky movements.

7. Bend quickly to the left three times.

Part III:

8. Finally, stretch your hands overhead again.

9. Reach down and touch your left hand to your right foot, and then return to the full-stretch position, with both hands extended overhead.

10.   Reach down and touch your right hand to your left foot, and return to the standing, full-stretch position.

11.   Repeat this third phase of the exercise six times, and work up to ten repetitions over a four-week period.

No. 14: The Big Bear Hug

In this highly effective exercise for toning up the arms and bust, you'll need a pair of three-pound dumbbells or a couple of heavy books or other items that you can hold easily in each hand. The motions for this exercise may sometimes remind you of reaching out in a broad, loving "bearhug" to gather into your arms a bunch of God's children.

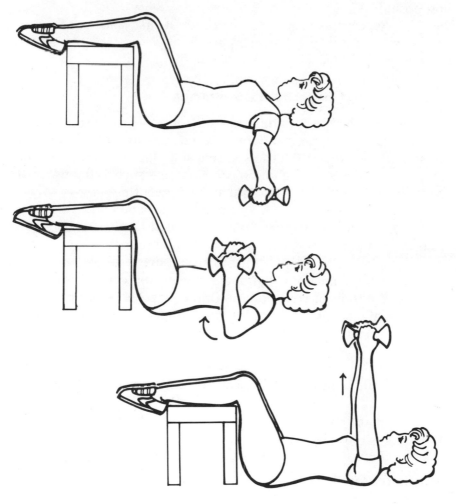

1.   Lie on the floor with your legs resting from the knees down on a bench or chair. Your arms should be extended out at ninety degrees to each side on the floor with palms up and a dumbbell in each hand.

2.   Bend your elbows slightly and raise the dumbbells to a position directly above your chest.

3.   Straighten your elbows, with the dumbbells still directly over your chest.

4.   Rotate the dumbbells by turning your palms outward.

5.   Slowly lower your arms to the floor.

6.   Rotate your hands again so that your palms are turned toward the ceiling and are placed under the dumbbells, in the starting position.

7.   Repeat this sequence five times at first, and work up to ten repetitions over a four-week period.

No. 15: Swimming

In this exercise for the arms and bust, which also requires dumbbells or equivalent weights, the movements are reminiscent of swimming strokes. On the spiritual side, I'm reminded of how important water is throughout the Scriptures—such as the water of baptism and the "living water" that Jesus says He will give to us.

1.   Lie with your back and head on a bench and your feet hanging off the end so that they are planted firmly on the floor. Your arms should be at your side, with a dumbbell in each hand. The dumbbells should be no heavier than five pounds!

2.   Slowly lift both dumbbells toward the ceiling in a wide arc over the front of your body until they reach a position behind you, directly out over the top of your head.

3.   Return your arms in a reverse arc back to the starting position.

4.   Move your left arm only in a similar sweeping arc until it's extended out behind you and positioned directly out over the top of your head.

5.   Return the left arm to the starting position, and repeat this motion with the right arm.

6.   Repeat this entire sequence five times at first, and work up to ten repetitions over a four- to six-week period.

As you can see, none of these exercises is particularly hard. You may have to do them regularly for a few weeks in order to build up the endurance to perform all fifteen straight through, without any rest periods in between.

As I mentioned at the beginning of this section, you may also find it helpful to do some sort of aerobic exercise that focuses on the legs, such as walking, jogging, or bicycling. When I'm walking, I often continue the same praying and meditating that I began during my stretch-and-strength exercises.

Whatever you do, it's important to make a commitment to stick with a regular program for at least a month. This means exercising regularly at least three to four times a week. Anything less won't help you build up a habit of exercise; also, it takes about a month for your body to adjust completely to a more rigorous lifestyle. For most people, there will be a few sore and aching muscles

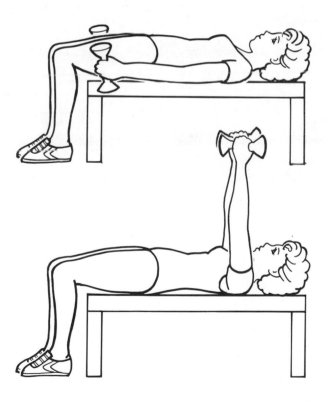

at first because of the challenge to muscles and ligaments that have been lying dormant for years.

It's likely you may find yourself focusing more on the physical than the spiritual during the first few weeks. But soon, you'll find the spiritual side of the experience becoming dominant. You'll realize that your decision to bring God into your exercise program is starting to stretch both your body and your spirit. The New You is beginning to emerge. You have embarked on a long-term exercise program that will greatly enhance your dieting efforts.

Now to the crux of the matter—the ten-week New You diet program that can make permanent weight loss a reality in your life.

CHAPTER FOUR

The Ten-Week New You Diet Program for Physical and Spiritual Health

I f a diet is going to work over a long period of time—that is, if you hope to take weight off and *keep* it off—it's necessary to see your intake of food in a different light. In the first place, it's essential to recognize the fundamental fact that you're both a physical and a spiritual being. Furthermore, you have to understand that the way you eat is directly connected with the way you relate to God Himself.

Remember: Your body is the temple of God, His chosen dwelling place on this earth. The way you maintain that "residence" through what you eat shows something about how much you value your relationship with the One who lives inside you.

The following seventy "diet days" have been designed with these principles in mind. Each morning you'll find it helpful to read the quoted Bible verse, the more extended Bible reference, and the devotional thought. Then, you might end with the suggested prayer or one of your own choosing. You know best what your deepest inner yearnings are and what God needs to show you to help you draw closer to Him.

After you've spent some time with these meditations, you'll be better prepared to embark upon the day's specific food program. Each of the diet days includes suggested diet menus for breakfast, lunch, dinner, and often a snack. All meals have been prepared by a professional nutritionist, and they are nutritionally balanced to ensure that the entire program is perfectly safe and effective.

You'll also find that the menus contain foods from all the major "food groups," including fruits, vegetables, dairy products, grain products, meats, and fats. Each day's dishes provide the proper balance of protein, complex carbohydrates, and fats. Of course, I've kept your fat intake especially low, because fats tend to be very high in calories and they aren't as good for you nutritionally as the other food types.

Finally, you should drink lots of water as a regular part of your daily diet. Specifically, it's important to drink eight eight-ounce glasses of water each day. I would suggest two glasses at each meal and two more during the middle of the day as "water snacks." The water is important for the basic health of your bodily systems and also helps keep your stomach full, thus reducing your craving for fattening foods.

There are approximately twelve hundred calories in each day's menus in the New You diet, or considerably less calories than most of us eat when left to our own devices. On the other hand, the calories are at a higher level than many more strict diets. I've chosen to keep the calorie values a little higher to enable you to keep your energy level up and to help you achieve a long-term change in your eating habits. The idea is to accomplish a steady, even if relatively small, weight loss each week. That's the healthiest way to reduce and to *keep* the pounds off.

If you faithfully follow the menus, you should lose at least two to five pounds a week, depending on your metabolism. Each item on the menus contains an indication of its approximate calorie values in parentheses. We have sometimes varied the calorie amounts for the same foods to give you a more realistic idea of your calorie intake. There will always be a range of calorie values rather than one firm calorie count because calorie counts depend on so many factors: quality of food, the brand, the amount, and how the food is prepared. If you want to substitute an item on one day's menus for an item from another day, be sure that the calorie values are about equal. Otherwise, you may find yourself getting too few or too many calories for a safe, effective diet.

As a special touch, I've included several dishes I use for meals that Pat, the rest of the family, and I have together. Some of these dishes are my favorites for entertaining. Yes, it *is* possible to entertain elegantly *and* stick to an effective diet plan! The recipes for these dishes, all of which have been marked by an asterisk (*), are contained in chapter 5.

As you begin this New You diet, don't forget what we discussed in the previous chapter on exercise. If you are naturally sedentary, it's important to increase the level of your physical activity even as you begin to cut down on the amount of food you consume. Otherwise, you may find you lose weight more slowly. Also, you will probably put it back on more quickly after you go off the diet.

Now, with these principles in mind, let's make today "Day One" of the New You!

Day 1

But those who wait on the LORD/Shall renew their strength;/They shall mount up with wings like eagles,/They shall run and not be weary,/They shall walk and not faint (Is. 40:31).

Read Isaiah 40:25–31.

Once, a friend of mine had an orchestra seat in the third row, center aisle, for a ballet. From this vantage point, she had an excellent view of the action on the stage. Entranced by the beautiful music and the graceful, swirling bodies before her, she didn't notice another advantage she had until the second act of the ballet began.

It was then she realized she could see into the wings adjoining the stage. She watched in fascination as the dancers prepared for their entries onto the stage. Each one breathed deeply in and out, in and out, with great concentration on each breath. Then suddenly, as the music struck the note that was a dancer's individual cue, he or she would burst upon the stage in a moment of glory.

You might say God gives us a special "cue" when our renewed energy shows us our health care is not in vain. In order to maintain this energy and to lose weight, I've learned over the years that I must follow a routine of regular exercise. But sometimes, even though the mind is willing, the body is weak. When I think I'm too tired to exercise, I turn to those words of the prophet Isaiah: I "wait" on God by focusing all my attention on Him for a few moments. Specifically, I concentrate on His scriptural promise and my hope in Him.

Prayer: Dear Father, thank You for caring about my physical strength and energy. Help me continue to keep my body fit so that I may carry out my daily tasks and my service for You with joy and vigor.

Breakfast:
  ¹/₂ cup blueberries, in season (45)
* 2 medium Love Waffles (180)
  1 cup skim milk (88)

Lunch:
  ¹/₂ roasted chicken breast (182)
  1 cup cooked carrots (40)
  1 slice whole wheat bread (61)

Dinner:
  1 halibut filet, broiled (214)
  1 stalk broccoli (47)
  1 slice cheddar cheese (139)
  1 baked potato, 1-2¹/₂ inches in diameter (76), with no
    butter, sour cream, or salt
  1 cup skim milk (88)

Snack:
  ¹/₂ cup mandarin orange pieces (42)

Remember: During the day, drink 8 8-ounce glasses of water.

---

*Items marked with an asterisk throughout this section have a corresponding recipe in chapter 5.

Day 2

I have treasured the words of His mouth more than my necessary food (Job 23:12).

Read Job 23:11–12.

Annette*, is one of the most overweight people I have ever met. She has tried all sorts of diets, some nutritionally sound and some not. Even with the aid and support of her doctors, she's been unsuccessful in her efforts to take off those unwanted pounds permanently.

It's true that at times she has lost as much as one hundred pounds. But her craving for food is so great that she gains the weight right back again—and sometimes she puts on a few extra inches for good measure.

Strangely enough, though, as often as I have eaten with people like Annette, I have never seen them overeat. I might never have known the basic problem except that one such person confessed to me the real reason for her downfall: she is a secret eater.

This person's desire for food is so great that sometimes in the middle of the night she gets out of bed and steals quietly into the kitchen. Though frequently not fully awake, she'll rummage through the refrigerator and start eating. Once, she even cooked herself the veal cutlets intended for the next evening's dinner. On top of that, she whipped up the corn and mashed potatoes to go with the main dish! Early another morning, she prepared and ate an entire box of macaroni and cheese.

Since this friend revealed her weakness, I decided I really had to share one of my own closely guarded confidences: I am often tempted to pilfer some high-calorie dish from the cupboard. Sometimes, I give in totally to the temptation; and when I do, believe me, I have a sweet tooth that won't be denied until the last jelly bean has been consumed!

I have discovered an antidote. When I yearn to put that sugar into my mouth, I now automatically turn to my Bible, open it to the book of Proverbs, and begin to read. At the same time, I ask the

---

*Names and specific details have been changed in the illustrations used throughout the book.

Lord to remove my desire for those sweets. It works! If we "treasure the words of His mouth," He'll deliver us from the cravings that enslave us.

Prayer: Dear God, I ask You to help me overcome the desires that have me in bondage. Fill me with Your Holy Spirit instead of food I don't need.

Breakfast:
   ¹/₂ cup grapefruit juice (48)
   1 slice whole wheat bread (61)
   2 tablespoons low-fat cottage cheese, or 1 poached egg (80)
   1 cup skim milk (88)

Lunch:
   Seafood special:
      2 ounces mixed seafood (124); broil in 2 teaspoons margarine (70); add ¹/₂ cup cooked tomato with onions, celery, and spinach (30); serve over ¹/₂ cup brown rice (88)

Dinner:
   3-ounce broiled veal chop (200)
   1 cup steamed carrots (40)
   1 teaspoon margarine (35)
* 1 Baked Apple (94)

Snack:
   1 cup orange and grapefruit sections (82)
   ¹/₂ cup diet ice cream (65)

Remember: During the day, drink 8 8-ounce glasses of water.

Day 3

If your brother is being injured by what you eat, you are no longer walking in love. Do not let what you eat cause the ruin of one for whom Christ died (Rom. 14:15 RSV).

Read Romans 14:14–22.

A friend of mine, on an outing with some friends, stopped for lunch with the group at a restaurant famous for its chili. They all ordered the chili except a young woman named Bev, who suffered from a form of colitis, an inflammation of the large intestine. Her doctor had told her to stay away from highly spiced foods, such as the chili the others were wolfing down. So she stuck to a safe but uninteresting item on the menu.

Everyone else was eating with gusto, except Bev who was just playing with her food, obviously not entirely satisfied. Then my friend, though aware of Bev's problem, devilishly urged her, "Bev, why don't you just taste a little of my chili?"

Bev did taste a little. Then she had a little more, and a little more. Minutes passed, and everything seemed to be fine. Suddenly, Bev shot up from the table and dashed toward the restroom.

My friend followed her and found her doubled over, in great pain. She immediately rushed her to the emergency room of a nearby hospital, where the doctor on duty gave her something to relieve her suffering.

"That was a sobering experience," my friend confided afterward. "I'll never urge food on anyone again!"

My friend's experience suggests a lesson we would all do well to learn. If someone is on a special diet for any reason, it's important to be supportive. And if we ourselves are on diets, it's helpful and advisable to spend more time with those who are sensitive to our needs and who keep temptation out of the way.

Prayer: Dear Lord, I ask You to help me love and care for others in a spirit of true fellowship. Make me sensitive to their needs so that I help, rather than hinder, them in developing good habits.

Breakfast:
  ¹/₂ cup orange juice (56)
  1 slice whole wheat toast (61)
  1 poached or boiled egg (80)
  1 cup skim milk (88)
           or
  ¹/₂ cup bran cereal (70)
  ¹/₂ cup fresh blueberries (45)
  1 cup skim milk (88)

Lunch:
  Turkey (or chicken), lettuce, and tomato sandwich (165):
    1 slice whole wheat bread (61); 1 slice turkey (or
    chicken breast) (40); ¹/₂ tomato (14); 1 tablespoon
    mayonnaise (50)
  1 cup skim milk (88)

Dinner:
  ¹/₂ broiled tarragon chicken breast (160) (Sprinkle tarragon
    lightly over chicken before broiling.)
  ¹/₂ cup noodles with poppy seeds (100)
  1 cup tossed salad with low-calorie dressing (20)

Snack:
  1 medium orange (60)
  1 cup skim milk (88)

Remember: During the day, drink 8 8-ounce glasses of water.

Day 4

Life is more than food, and the body is more than clothing (Luke 12:23).

Read Luke 12:22–26.

We all know people who talk about food or clothes to the ex-
clusion of everything else. Women seem to be the offenders in
many cases, though some men may fall into this trap as well, especially if they happen to be on diets!

How can we be witnesses for our dear Lord when all we talk
about is food or clothes? Is the exchange of recipes *really* uplifting
conversation? Does this sort of discussion glorify Jesus? No more
than our fat bodies do!

Constant talk of food certainly doesn't make us more interesting, vital people to be around. It just makes us "hungrier." We need
to read and study to develop other interests. Perhaps a class in
handicrafts or pottery will help. If you decide to develop a hobby,
you might try something you've always wanted to do, as I did just a
few months ago.

I went to a smocking class and learned a useful skill I had always been interested in but somehow had never had time to develop. As a result, now I have a new craft, and you should see my
granddaughters! Another benefit of handwork—one I didn't plan
on but was pleasantly surprised to discover—is that you can't eat
while you are doing it!

To keep your mind and hands off food and on more productive pursuits, you might also get involved in community activities.
For example, do volunteer work in hospitals, in your church, for
your favorite political candidate, or at a center for special children.
Get some interests other than eating! Then, you'll be on the road to
becoming the person Jesus wants you to be.

Prayer: Dear Lord, help me to be the person You created me
to be. Guide and direct me to new paths of interest and service.
Keep my mind away from food, and help me to glorify You in all
that I do.

Breakfast:
   1 cup orange juice (112)
* Omelet (one egg), with assorted cheese or vegetable
      toppings (92)
   Coffee or tea, no cream or sugar

Lunch:
   3 ounces baked shad (170)
   ¹/₂ cup steamed broccoli (30)
   ¹/₂ cup summer squash (14)
   1 cup skim milk (88)
* 1 cup Minted Fresh Fruit (84)

Dinner:
* 3 ounces Skewered Lamb (199)
   1 boiled ear of corn (70)
* ¹/₂ cup Cucumber-Mint Salad (23)
* ¹/₄ cup Spanish Cream (76)
   1 cup skim milk (88)
   Coffee or tea, no cream or sugar

Snack:
   1 apple (86)

Remember: During the day, drink 8 8-ounce glasses of water.

Day 5

Do not be carried about with various and strange doctrines. For it is good that the heart be established by grace, not with foods which have not profited those who have been occupied with them (Heb. 13:9).

Read Hebrews 13:7–9.

We all know people who have tried one diet after another. Maybe you are one of them. Sometimes, certain individuals become unbalanced in pursuing their food programs; instead of consuming the diets, the diets begin to consume them. They eat them; they talk about them; they prepare them; they *live* them. The diet regimen has in effect "eaten them up," and there is no room for anything else, including the Lord.

What is true of strange doctrines is also true of strange diets. Just as our Lord didn't come into this world to make us all fanatics, obsessed with doing bizarre things, neither did He intend for us to eat in strange ways!

The secret to any successful diet lies not in radical nutrition theories but in the quantities consumed. Less meat and more vegetables, for one thing! If you can, imagine three people ordering one steak and then dividing it three ways: That's the amount of steak you should eat, maybe once a week.

Whatever diet program you choose, you should eat a normal, well-balanced menu, including the "basic four" food types. That is, you need milk, meat, fruits and vegetables, and whole grains every day. This is balanced nutrition for a balanced life!

Prayer: Lord Jesus, help me to be balanced in all things that I might be a witness to Your power and glory. Guard me from strange diets as well as strange doctrines. Help me to serve You in every way possible.

Breakfast:
* 6-ounce glass Tomato Ice (32)
  $^1/_2$ cup bran cereal (70)
  $^1/_2$ cup blueberries (45)
  $^1/_2$ cup skim milk (44)
  Coffee or tea, no cream or sugar

Lunch:
  $3^1/_2$ ounces tuna fish, canned in water (127)
  $^1/_2$ cup snap beans (30)
  1 medium baked potato (76)
  1 cup skim milk (88)

Dinner:
* 1 serving Wild Rice Casserole (150)
* $^1/_2$ cup Ratatouille (50)
* 1 cup French Carrot Salad (48)
* $^1/_2$ cup Red, White, and Blue Dessert (40)
  Coffee or tea, no cream or sugar

Snack:
  1 cup skim milk (88)

Remember: During the day, drink 8 8-ounce glasses of water.

Day 6

For the kingdom of God is not food and drink, but righteousness and peace and joy in the Holy Spirit (Rom. 14:17).

Read Romans 14:17–18.

It was Richie's first opportunity to sit at the long Thanksgiving dinner table, with all the family and friends gathered around. He was three years old. How his eyes sparkled when he saw the beautiful selection of food, with the colorful centerpiece and the shining silver, china, and crystal. He exclaimed delightedly over the little Indian with his name on it that marked his place at the table.

His mother and grandmother set out platters of delicious-smelling food, and the family bowed their heads and joined their hands to say grace. Richie was fairly bursting with excitement and could hardly sit still in his seat.

When the blessing was over and the food began to be passed around, he leaned forward and called to the head of the table, "Grandpa, could we do the 'amens' again?"

The family laughed, but they did murmur a few extra "amens." Then, they turned their attention back to their plates. Much later, when it was time to leave, Richie said his thank-yous to his grandparents and was about to go. Suddenly, he turned back and said, "The best part was the 'amens.' "

So it should be for all of us. It would make dieting so much easier if at holiday times we could just let the joy of God's many blessings fill us—instead of stuffing ourselves with food. At parties, let's begin to enjoy the pleasure of being with other people. Let's take part in conversations and rejoice in the fact that God has granted us this time with friends and loved ones.

Prayer: Most bountiful God, help me to feast on the peace and joy of being with those whom I love rather than just on my food.

Breakfast:
   $1/2$ grapefruit (55)
   $1/2$ toasted soya muffin (68), with
   2 tablespoons dietetic strawberry spread (24)
   1 cup skim milk (88)
   Coffee or tea, no cream or sugar

Lunch:
* 1 cup Minted Fresh Fruit (84)
   Special tossed salad (175):
      1 cup mixed iceberg lettuce, romaine, spinach, mush-
      rooms, tomatoes, and 1 hard-boiled egg, with low-calorie
      dressing
* 1 slice Surprise Bread (119)
   Coffee or tea, no cream or sugar

Dinner:
   3 ounces broiled veal, with mushrooms (210)
* $1/4$ cup cooked Brown and Wild Rice (44)
   $1/2$ cup mixed vegetables (58)
   1 cup tossed green salad (20) with
   1 teaspoon oil and vinegar dressing (35)
   1 cup skim milk (88)
   Coffee or tea, no cream or sugar

Snack:
   1 medium apple (86)

Remember: During the day, drink 8 8-ounce glasses of water.

Day 7

Therefore let no one judge you in food or in drink, or regarding a festival or a new moon or sabbaths (Col. 2:16).

Read Colossians 2:16–19.

A twenty-three-year-old bachelor, who had just arrived in New York City from a small town in the Midwest, wanted to impress a woman he had just met. He took her to dine at a fancy, expensive restaurant. After they had been seated, the waiter presented them with the menus, returned a few minutes later, and murmured, "Would the gentleman care to order for himself and the lady?"

The young man could tell he was in over his head because most of the dishes were in a foreign language; furthermore, he had no idea what the ones in English were about. Worried now that he would look like a fool in front of his companion, he decided to order artichokes as an appetizer—"because that was one of the few things on the menu I could pronounce. Actually, I had never seen an artichoke, much less eaten one."

The artichokes finally arrived, but they didn't resemble any other food he had ever seen—unless it was some sort of soft, green pineapple. "I didn't have the faintest idea how to eat it," he recalls. "My eyes darted around the room in an effort to see if anyone else was eating one of the things. Finally, I saw somebody with the same order: he pulled out a leaf, dipped it in the sauce that had been provided, and then put it in his mouth."

Our bachelor followed suit—except that he failed to note that the other patron had scraped off the soft outside of the artichoke with his teeth and then taken the leaf out of his mouth. The young man popped the entire leaf in his mouth and tried to chew it, with unsuccessful results. At this point, the waiter came over and gave him a demonstration of how to eat artichokes.

"I was totally embarrassed and so was my date," he says. "I felt that everyone was staring at me, and the entire evening was ruined. I never took that woman out again, either."

Sometimes, food can become a status symbol as we try to show others our sophistication. But I believe God doesn't want us to judge or be judged on any basis, certainly not by the food we eat. If food has its proper place in our lives, it's easy just to say, "I've never eaten this before—what do I do with it?" Seeking to impress others only serves to separate us from one another and may well impair relationships. When we put our food in proper perspective, it can contribute to a convivial atmosphere that enhances friendships.

Prayer: Lord, help me to be humble, as Your Son Jesus was. Teach me to use food for the nourishment of my body and not my ego.

Breakfast:
* 6-ounce glass Tomato Ice (35)
* 2 Love Waffles (180)
  1/2 cup skim milk (44)
  Coffee or tea, no cream or sugar

Lunch:
  3 ounces broiled steak (260)
  1 cup tossed salad (20)
  1 teaspoon oil and vinegar dressing (35)

Dinner:
* 1 1/2 ounces Shrimp Mousse (95)
* 3 ounces Swedish Meat Balls (318)
  1 cup spinach (48)
  4 Ritz crackers (68)
  Coffee or tea, no cream or sugar

Snack:
* 6 ounces Fruit Punch (40)

Remember: During the day, drink 8 8-ounce glasses of water.

Day 8

Along the bank of the river, on this side and that, will grow all kinds of trees used for food; their leaves will not wither, and their fruit will not fail. They will bear fruit every month, because their water flows from the sanctuary. Their fruit will be for food, and their leaves for medicine (Ezek. 47:12).

Read Ezekiel 47:7–12.

A nutritionist, who was being interviewed on one of the popular TV talk shows, was asked by an interviewer, "Once I've lost weight, how can I keep it off?"

"There's at least one easy rule to follow," the expert said. "Avoid eating sauces on foods."

In today's Bible reading, we see that God made some similar provisions for good nutrition and weight maintenance. He says He will make available for His people fresh fruit, as well as fresh fish, but there's no suggestion that these natural foods should be served with high-calorie sauces.

Most of us are so accustomed to canned foods or entrees soaked in sauces that we've forgotten how glorious the taste of the unadorned dish can really be. As God's children, let's try the simple diet suggested in the words of His prophet and see how much easier it is to keep those pounds off after we've reached a lower weight.

Prayer: Dear God, help me to change my eating habits and begin to see *Your* meal plan in the fresh, simple foods You have provided for me.

Breakfast:
 ¹/₂ grapefruit (55)
* 2 Love Waffles (180)
 ¹/₂ cup skim milk (44)
 Coffee or tea, no cream or sugar

Lunch:
* 1 cup Minted Fresh Fruit (84)
  3¹/₂ ounces tuna, in water (127)
  ³/₄ cup mixed vegetables (87)
  ¹/₂ cup plain, low-fat yogurt (71), sprinkled with
     blueberries (15)

Dinner:
* 1 cup Asparagus Consommé (70)
* 3 ounces Beef Wellington (250)
* 1 Broiled Tomato Cup, filled with chopped spinach (30)
* 1 Potato Ball (40)
* ¹/₂ Grapefruit-Avocado Salad, with pomegranate seeds (50)
  Coffee or tea, no cream or sugar

Snack:
* 1 Poached Pear in Red Wine* (100)

Remember: During the day, drink 8 8-ounce glasses of water.

---

*Several recipes in chapter 5 call for wine or cooking sherry. Keep in mind that all alcoholic content is dissipated through the cooking process.

Day 9

Therefore I say to you, do not worry about your life, what you will eat or what you will drink; nor about your body, what you will put on. Is not life more than food and the body more than clothing? (Matt. 6:25).

Read Matthew 6:25–34.

Jan, a single woman, had invited a very dear married couple to her apartment for dinner. Although she had been to their place many times, her friends had never visited Jan, primarily because they lived outside the city and were completely occupied in raising their five children.

Now that they had finally arranged their schedules so that they could visit her, Jan was quite anxious to be certain that everything was perfect. She spent all of Friday evening cleaning her apartment. Then, she got up early Saturday morning, the day of the big event, and began to prepare the meal.

She had chosen to cook a Chinese pepper steak, and that meant laying out a variety of specially selected ingredients and then putting them into a slow cooker to simmer for eight hours. It was definitely going to be an all-day affair, but everything seemed to be going quite smoothly.

When Jan's company arrived exactly on time late that afternoon, they "oohed" and "aahed" over her apartment, as good friends often do when they appreciate the taste and hard work that go into proper home decoration and cleaning. Then, the three went out for a walk along a nearby river so that they could enjoy Jan's lovely neighborhood before dinner.

They returned with hearty appetites, and the visiting couple immediately went to the dining room table, which Jan had already set with her best china and glassware. Jan headed into the kitchen—and when she entered, she almost had a heart attack: She had forgotten to plug in the cooker!

"There was nothing to do but go out and confess my stupidity to my friends," Jan says. "One look at my face, and they jumped up from their seats and gathered me in their arms. Even as I was on the verge of tears, they were laughing and assuring me of their love."

Jan had to send out for pizza that evening, but she and the

couple were never closer in their friendship than they were that evening. In an unforgettable way, Jan had learned that, ultimately, we give and receive love not through the quality of the food we serve, but through the way we respond to others in need. Indeed, unconditional love—love that God Himself makes available to us despite our mistakes and follies—is really what life is all about.

Prayer: Lord, I thank You for the unconditional love You have shown me through Your Son Jesus Christ. Help me to live each day secure in the knowledge of what You have done for me in Him. Help me to remember the enormity of Your love when I am tempted to eat those goodies I must not eat. Your love is sufficient!

Breakfast:
    ¹/₂ cup strawberries (26)
    ¹/₂ cup bran cereal (70)
    1 cup skim milk (88)

Lunch:
    3¹/₂ ounces broiled swordfish (174)
    1 cup mixed vegetables (116)
*   ³/₄ cup Bulgur Salad (90)
    ¹/₂ cup fruit mix (31)

Dinner:
    ¹/₂ chicken breast, boiled, baked, or broiled (160)
    1 cup snap beans (60)
*   ¹/₄ cup cooked Brown and Wild Rice (44)
    ¹/₂ cup plain, low-fat yogurt, with slivers of cinnamon
      apples (85)

Snack:
    1 cup skim milk (88)
    ¹/₄ cantaloupe (41)

Remember: During the day, drink 8 8-ounce glasses of water.

Day 10

So continuing daily with one accord in the temple, and breaking bread from house to house, they ate their food with gladness and simplicity of heart (Acts 2:46).

Read Acts 2:42–47.

A church youth leader organized a very special night for her teen-age charges—even though it seemed at one point they might be courting a culinary disaster. The youth group had decided to sponsor a spaghetti dinner for the entire congregation, and as part of the event the leader invited a gifted young musician, Bill, to lead the group in songs.

An unusually large crowd showed up for the event; and since dinner had been planned first, they all seated themselves at the tables and waited with anticipation for the feast they had been promised.

But all was not well in the kitchen.

The teen-agers, as well as the youth leader, were complete amateurs when it came to cooking for large numbers of people. First of all, most of the guests had arrived before the water had even been poured and boiled for the spaghetti. Then, in the rush to begin serving, nobody rinsed the pasta after it had drained. The cooks were left with a sticky, gooey mess, which they had to try to salvage for the hungry hordes outside. Finally, after a considerable struggle, they managed to get everybody served and fed.

Then came the highlight of the evening: Bill sang some of his favorite numbers and then, with the teen-agers, led the entire group in hymns and spiritual folk songs. The youngsters and Bill conveyed the music with such sincerity that everyone was deeply touched. The Spirit was moving that evening in a way that was rare and beautiful.

The pastor, with tears in his eyes, offered a prayer of gratitude at the end of the festivities. It was one of that church's finest moments, despite the clumsiness of the serving and the texture of the spaghetti. There were echoes of the best mealtimes of the New Testament Christian community in this event—a sense of gladness and sincerity in the new faith that brought hope and joy to their lives.

Those dieters who can capture some of this atmosphere may

find themselves experiencing a moving of the Spirit at their own mealtimes. When this happens, they are likely to focus less on the food they are eating and more on the total, joyful experience of breaking bread together.

Prayer: Dear Lord, help me to look upon the breaking of bread with others as incidental to the joy and gladness of being with them in Your presence, as we praise You and have fellowship together.

Breakfast:
　　1 cup dry bran cereal (unsweetened) (140)
　　1 cup skim milk (88)
　　1/2 cup fresh black raspberries (49)

Lunch:
　　3 1/2 ounces flounder, baked or broiled (202)
　　1/2 cup mixed vegetables (58)
　　1 sliced orange with 2 tablespoons of plain,
　　　　low-fat yogurt (79)

Dinner:
*　1 cup Asparagus Consommé (70)
　　1 broiled, 3 1/2-ounce lamb chop (237)
　　3/4 cup broccoli, with 1 teaspoon lemon butter (93)
*　1 Potato Ball (40)
*　1/2 cup Grapefruit-Avocado Salad (50)
*　1 Poached Pear in Red Wine (100)
　　1/2 cup skim milk (44)
　　Coffee or tea, no cream or sugar

Snack:
*　1 cup Fruit Punch (40)

Remember: During the day, drink 8 8-ounce glasses of water.

Day 11

Do not mix with winebibbers,/Or with gluttonous eaters of meat;/For the drunkard and the glutton will come to poverty,/And drowsiness will clothe a man with rags (Prov. 23:20–21).

Read Proverbs 23:19–21.

Is there anyone who hasn't experienced that horrible feeling that comes with eating or drinking too much? With many people, too much food or almost any amount of alcohol will produce a drowsiness that causes just one overriding thought: "I wish I could find a place to lay down my head!"

One young woman went out on a date with her boyfriend and his family on his college graduation day. She was a nondrinker, but the father ordered champagne for everyone, and the young woman was afraid she would spoil things if she didn't join in. She accepted the glass that was offered to her and participated in all the toasts.

The effects were immediate. She still has a vivid recollection of what she wore on that occasion because even today she can see in her mind's eye the polka dots on her dress dancing before her as she stared down into her lap. She tried to sit up straight, but her feet kept sliding away. Then, she tried to eat, but the food somehow evaded her fork.

Someone finally noticed her predicament and gently escorted her to the rest room, where she splashed cold water on her face. Actually, what she really wanted to do was go directly home, climb into bed, and go to sleep. That was exactly what she did immediately after the dinner was finished.

A potentially lovely and festive occasion was ruined for this young woman, who confused eating and drinking with being sociable. Most people at parties will never notice how much we eat or drink—unless we consume too much. On the other hand, over the long haul they *will* notice how the unsightly extra calories are piling up on our bodies if we insist on consuming the hollow calories of alcohol or the extra helpings of rich foods that are placed before us at special dinners.

Prayer: Dear Lord, teach me moderation in all things. Give me the strength to abstain from that which will harm my body and befuddle my senses.

Breakfast:
   ¹/₂ cantaloupe (6-inch melon) (82)
   1 soft-cooked egg (80)
   1 slice whole wheat toast (61)
   1 cup skim milk (88)
   Coffee or tea, no cream or sugar

Lunch:
   Broiled cheese and tomato sandwich (204):
      1 ounce cheese (107)
      ¹/₂ whole wheat English muffin (65)
      1¹/₂ fresh tomato on top (38)
   1 cup skim milk (88)

Dinner:
   4 ounces spiced, unsweetened apple juice (58)
   3 ounces broiled red snapper (182)
* 1 Broiled Tomato Cup, filled with Petite Pois (30)
* 1 Potato Ball (40)
* 1 cup Grapefruit-Avocado Salad, with pomegranate seeds and
      Fruit Dip (50)
   1 cup fresh black raspberries (98), over crushed ice
   Coffee or tea, no cream or sugar

Snack:
   2 pieces Melba toast (60)

Remember: During the day, drink 8 8-ounce glasses of water.

Day 12

Nevertheless He did not leave Himself without witness, in that He did good, gave us rain from heaven and fruitful seasons, filling our hearts with food and gladness (Acts 14:17).

Read Acts 14:8–18.

Little miracles seem to be happening all around us these days, and some even involve food. I'm not aware of anything quite like the feeding of the five thousand by Jesus. But a friend of mine is involved in a small-group experience where God is clearly at work in setting up the menu, just as the Son of God did on those Galilean hillsides.

Many of the members of his church have joined what they call "extended families," or groups of about ten or twelve people who meet regularly for dinner in one of the members' homes. "But nothing is ever planned in advance, as far as the food is concerned," he says. "Although we all bring something to be shared, nobody reveals the identity of his dish to anyone else."

Among some of the people at these dinners, especially the newcomers, there may be a moment of anxiety at the last minute, a worry that "this time, folks, we're going to have all desserts or all salads or all main dishes!" But that never happens. Amazingly, there's always a balanced meal, and there's always more than enough to go around.

"We kind of feel that we're leaving it up to the Spirit to plan our menu," my friend says.

Perhaps the key to this phenomenon is the fact that the focus is not on the food, but on the presence of the Lord at each meal. He ties together these believers as they share their concerns and thoughts and pray with one another. They are joyful at gatherings, not because of the food but because they are recognizing God as the ultimate source of satisfaction and nourishment in their lives.

Prayer: Dear Lord, help me to experience more the joy of being with good friends. Show me the most meaningful way to share the earthly abundance You have given me.

Breakfast:
   $^1/_2$ cup orange juice (56)
   1 slice French toast (119)
   $^1/_2$ cup plain, low-fat yogurt, with slivers of cinnamon
      apples (85)
   $^1/_2$ cup skim milk (44)
   Coffee or tea, no cream or sugar

Lunch:
   3 ounces broiled sirloin steak (260)
   1 cup steamed cabbage (32)
   1 cup green beans (60)
   1 teaspoon margarine (35)
   1 slice whole wheat bread (61)
   $^1/_2$ cup skim milk (44)

Dinner:
   $^1/_2$ roasted chicken breast (182)
   1 cup steamed broccoli (58)
   1 cup summer squash (29)
   $^1/_2$ cup watermelon (32)
   1 cup skim milk (88)

Snack:
   $^1/_2$ slice banana bread (67), with 1 tablespoon cream
      cheese (48)

Remember: During the day, drink 8 8-ounce glasses of water.

Day 13

Be anxious for nothing, but in everything by prayer and supplication, with thanksgiving, let your requests be made known to God (Phil. 4:6).

Read Philippians 4:4–17.

I once counseled a young woman who was on a diet to ask God for help in sticking to it. But she replied, "I believe in prayer, but I think in the last analysis, this matter of reducing is up to me. I really don't think God is interested in hearing about the minute details of my life. He has more important things to deal with than the size of my tummy or the number of pounds I weigh."

Is that really true?

I knew, for example, that this woman was deeply concerned about her weight because she was in the midst of job interviews, and she knew she didn't look her best. She was at least twenty pounds overweight, and the clothes that used to look so sharp on her didn't fit any more. As a result, she lacked confidence in herself and in her ability to project an attractive image to the corporate officials she was scheduled to see.

We often hesitate to "bother" God with what seem to be the little things in our lives because we think He is too busy; or we somehow think it's "un-Christian" to ask for something for ourselves; or we simply don't believe God will ever answer prayers that are so completely personal.

But God *does* want to be "bothered." He does care about the little things in our lives because He knows—as we know, if we're really honest with ourselves—that the seemingly little things may affect us in the biggest ways.

The young woman may have told me her weight problem was small, but she knew, down deep, that it was really the most important thing in the world to her at that moment. Those extra pounds were a great source of anxiety for her, and that was a sure signal that she should have put the matter before God in prayer. Not only that, even as she made this request in prayer, it would have been quite appropriate for her to thank Him with the assurance He would answer.

Prayer: Dear God, I ask You to strengthen me in my resolve to lose weight. Make me strong enough to resist the temptation to eat the wrong things. Help me change my eating habits now and for all time.

Breakfast:
* * 1 cup Bird Seed Cereal (110)
  1 cup strawberries (52)
  1 cup skim milk (88)

Lunch:
  3½ ounces broiled flounder (202)
  1 cup mixed vegetables (116)
  ½ cup mixed fruit (31)
  10 cherries (13)
  1 cup skim milk (88)

Dinner:
  3 ounces ground beef patty (235)
  6-ounce glass tomato juice (35)
  ½ cup snap beans (30)
* * ¼ cup cooked Brown and Wild Rice (44)
  1 cup skim milk (88)

Snack:
  1 slice medium pineapple, fresh or canned
    in its own juice (88)
  ½ cup strawberry milk (½ cup skim milk, with 1 teaspoon
    strawberry jam) (61)

Remember: During the day, drink 8 8-ounce glasses of water.

Day 14

Rejoice always, pray without ceasing, in everything give thanks; for this is the will of God in Christ Jesus for you (1 Thess. 5:16–18).

Read 1 Thessalonians 5:16–24.

A number of years ago, a man I know became fascinated by the challenge of achieving constant or continuous prayer. He had been reading a book by J. D. Salinger in which the young heroine was taken with the practice of some Russian monks, who had reportedly found they were able to control their heartbeats by chanting.

My friend began to experiment with a variety of techniques including various traditional devotional approaches, a style of monastic meditation, and even mechanical biofeedback methods. His main goal seemed to be to make his mind and body enter some superspiritual state in record-breaking time.

This goal of becoming some sort of spiritual sage continued for a few months—perhaps even as long as a year. After failing to see any progress in acquiring great powers, he lost interest and turned his attention toward finding the ultimate "high" in aerobic exercise.

It saddened me to watch the rise and fall of enthusiasm in this young man, especially since I felt that his quest for God's blessings had some merit. His problem was that he was looking for a quick, dramatic answer to problems that require the slow and steady building of a deep, personal relationship with the Lord.

As I've matured, I've found I no longer look for mysterious incantations to improve my inner life just as I don't look for magical, overnight solutions to a weight problem. I realize now that the only way to take weight off safely and permanently is to do it bit by bit, on a regular daily basis. Then, at the end of several weeks or months, I may look at myself in a mirror and realize, "Hey, I've really made some progress with that steady, step-by-step program."

It's a similar process as we try to grow closer to God. I have learned it's essential to make Him a regular part of my prayer life early in the morning. If I have time for an hour of Bible reading and prayer, that's great. If I can only spare thirty minutes or even fifteen minutes on some mornings, that's all right too. The key is doing *something* with the Lord on a daily basis. That puts me in an attitude of prayer for the rest of the day and makes me more likely to consult Him on the spur of the moment, when daily challenges arise.

Prayer: Lord, help me to search out Your will for my life through prayer. Show me how I should pray to give me greater commitment and discipline in my efforts to lose weight.

Breakfast:
    1 cup wheat flakes (110)
    1 cup fresh strawberries (52)
    1 cup skim milk (88)

Lunch:
    3 ounces broiled veal (200)
    1 cup mixed vegetables (116)
    6-ounce glass tomato juice (35)

Dinner:
    3 1/2 ounces turkey breast (176)
    1/2 cup snap beans (30)
*   1/4 cup cooked Brown and Wild Rice (44)
    1 teaspoon butter (35)
    1/2 cup red raspberries, in Diet Jello or DeZerta (55)
    1 cup skim milk (88)

Snack:
    1 slice medium pineapple (88)

Remember: During the day, drink 8 8-ounce glasses of water.

Day 15

Woe to men mighty at drinking wine,/Woe to men valiant
for mixing intoxicating drink (Is. 5:22).

Read Isaiah 5:22–33.

There are at least three levels on which alcohol is a major enemy to any diet.

On the first level, nearly every responsible diet program recommends reduction or elimination of alcohol intake because it involves a nonnutritious consumption of calories—or "hollow" or "empty" calories, as some experts have put it. In other words, when you drink, you always have to add extra foods to achieve a healthy balance of protein, complex carbohydrates, and fats, because alcohol doesn't add any important nutrients to your diet.

There is a second and more serious level of problems with alcohol: the area of human relationships. If you hope to take off weight and keep it off, it's essential that you feel right about yourself and your relationships with others. The more frustrated you feel in these areas, the more likely you are to try to forget your troubles in food and drink.

A friend of mine illustrates this point through a story from her childhood. It seems that her father was an alcoholic, though she didn't realize this fact until she got older. When she was a very young child, he would act very happy and "crazy" around her. Also, he would make all kinds of wonderful promises, which she believed without reservation. Then time after time, none of the toys or trips ever materialized. She eventually no longer believed her father.

A serious problem developed as this girl got older. She became cynical about life in general. She had learned not to believe in anybody or anything—including God. She became hard and sarcastic. She seemed unable to find satisfaction in anything in life. In an ironic continuation of the very personality problem that had flawed her early relationship with her father, she turned to her own version of his solution. She not only drank too much alcohol, but she also indulged too freely in desserts and snacks. Among other things, she steadily put on excess weight.

Finally, God broke through this woman's defensive, crusty exterior. When the gospel was presented in an attractive way to her by a close friend, she made a commitment to Christ. But even after her conversion, it took time and prayer for her to forget her disappointment in her father and believe in people again.

On a third and final level—perhaps the most important of all for the dieter—alcohol attacks our wills. The first step in losing weight is to make a decision to embark on an effective program. The second step is to establish a regular, well-disciplined approach to eating and exercise. Yet both of these steps require acts of the will, an inner capacity and strength which is usually seriously impaired when alcohol comes into the picture.

Prayer: Father, strengthen my will power. Show me the way to escape when I am confronted with temptation.

Breakfast:
   1 cup skim milk (88)
   1 cup bran cereal (140)
   1/2 cup fresh blueberries (45)
   Coffee or tea, no cream or sugar

Lunch:
   1 cup St. John's Salad (111)
   Recipe for two cups:
   1 diced medium apple (86)
   10 sprigs watercress (2)
   1/2 cup raspberries (49)
   6 leaves of lettuce and carrot slivers (6)
   1 tablespoon sweet oil (35)
   1 tablespoon honey, dash of lemon juice, and paprika (35)
   1 cup skim milk (88)

Dinner:
   3 ounces mixed seafood (haddock, halibut, codfish) (160)
   1/4 cup mixed vegetables (29)
   1 cup tossed salad, with dash of vinegar (20)
   1 wedge medium honeydew melon (41)
   1 cup skim milk (88)

Snack:
  $^{1}/_{2}$ banana (42)
  $^{1}/_{2}$ cup skim milk (44)

Remember: During the day, drink 8 8-ounce glasses of water.

Day 16

The Lord's people grew rich, but rebellious; they were fat and stuffed with food. They abandoned God their Creator and rejected their mighty savior (Deut. 32: 15 TEV).

Read Deuteronomy 32:13–18.

I remember suffering once from a very sore jaw as a result of dental surgery. My dentist had laid down a strict program of dental hygiene to help me heal quickly and get back to normal. The program he had prescribed was quite time-consuming, but anything was worth ending the agony and discomfort I was facing.

In a few days my mouth had healed nicely. But as my jaw returned to normal, my zeal for cleaning my teeth according to the dentist's instructions began to fade. Then, I had a flare-up of the problem because I wasn't cleaning my mouth properly. I returned to following the letter of the dentist's law until I was completely well again.

Moses said that essentially the same thing happened to the children of Israel. When they were homeless and suffering, they called upon God to help them and they obeyed His commandments to the letter. But after He brought them into the Promised Land and caused them to prosper, they didn't worship God with the same zeal they had once displayed. In many cases, they completely forgot or ignored His wishes and even turned to the worship of other gods.

A similar set of principles seems to apply to those who are on diets. As we struggle to achieve the loss of the first ten or twenty pounds, we stick with our diets because we have some definite goal in mind: We know we want to be in better health; or perhaps we want to fit into those bathing suits we used to wear, years ago.

After we are successful in losing those first pounds, others begin to notice approvingly and we bask in their compliments. We start to get the feeling that we've finally arrived, that we've recaptured the slim figures of our youth.

This is a most dangerous moment because it's easy to become complacent. It's easy to forget that the same vigilance and commitment are as necessary to maintain a lower weight as to arrive at it in the first place. It's all too easy to lose, in short order, what you've struggled so hard to achieve. It's easy, that is, unless you make a lifelong commitment to change your eating habits.

Prayer: Lord, thank You for helping me lose the weight I've already lost—and the additional weight I know I'm going to lose. But help me guard against complacency in my weight loss program.

Breakfast:
    1 cup grapefruit juice (96)
*   1 cup Bird Seed Cereal (110)
    1 cup skim milk (88)
    1 cup strawberries (52)

Lunch:
*   1 cup Chili with Beans (175)
    8 spears asparagus (26)
    1/2 cup plain, low-fat yogurt, with blueberries (85)

Dinner:
    1/2 chicken breast, roasted (182)
    1 baked potato, 1-2 1/2 inches in diameter (76), with no butter
      or sour cream
    1 cup mixed vegetables (116)
    1 cup skim milk (88)

Snack:
    1 cup unsweetened fruit cocktail (91)

Remember: During the day, drink 8 8-ounce glasses of water.

Day 17

Why do you kick at My sacrifice and My offering which I have commanded in My habitation, and honor your sons more than Me, to make yourselves fat with the best of all the offerings of Israel My people? (1 Sam. 2:29).

Read 1 Samuel 2:27–36.

Do you remember as a child the awful temptation—when a plate of cookies was being passed, or when some scrumptious cake was being served—to take the biggest piece? It seemed as though your eyes darted about with a will of their own to seek out the largest portion. You tentatively reached out your hand, while your mother's voice echoed in your mind, if not in your ear: "Don't be greedy! Don't grab the biggest one for yourself!"

Sometimes, the warning was strong enough to stop your hand midway in the air and redirect you to a smaller piece. But other times, greed won out.

In today's Bible reading, God punishes Eli, the high priest, for permitting his sons to be greedy. Eli had received animal sacrifices for God, but he had allowed his sons to take the choicest portions of meat for themselves. As a result, God severed His relationship with Eli and his descendants.

Greediness is a serious shortcoming, a serious act of rebellion against the moral order God has established. If we express our greed on the grand scale, as Eli's sons did, our very relationship with God may be placed in jeopardy. If we are greedy in the little things of life, there are often other unpleasant consequences.

Adults who always go for the second helping or for the largest piece of dessert are doing more than just reverting to childish expressions of mealtime greed. They're also storing up negative consequences in their bodies in the form of calories—calories which will turn to pounds, and pounds which will sap energy and increase the risk of serious health problems.

So now that you're grown up, replace the voice of your mother in your mind with the voice of God: "Why then look with greedy eye...?"

Prayer: Dear God, thank You for loving me enough to teach

me how to give up my childish greed and leave the biggest portions
for others.

Breakfast:
 ¹/₂ cup apple juice (58)
 1 soft-boiled egg (80)
 ¹/₂ cup skim milk (44)
 1 slice whole wheat toast (61)

Lunch:
 Special toasted sandwich:
   1 slice whole wheat bread (61)
   6 lettuce leaves (4)
   2 slices tomato (26)
 ¹/₂ cup cottage cheese (80)
 2 pear halves (100)

Dinner:
 2 ounces beef, au jus, roasted and sliced (230)
 ¹/₄ cup mashed potatoes (44)
 1 cup raw cauliflower, with touch of mustard sauce (35)
* 1 cup Green Salad (20)
 1 tablespoon mayonnaise dressing (35)
 1 cup orange slices and spiced peaches (70)

Snack:
 ¹/₂ cantaloupe (82)
 ¹/₂ cup blueberries (45)

Remember: During the day, drink 8 8-ounce glasses of water.

Day 18

The Lord Almighty is going to send disease to punish those who are now well-fed. In their bodies will be a fire that burns and burns (Is. 10:16 TEV).

Read Isaiah 10:13–19.

A friend of mine has an aunt who has never learned to curb her appetite. As the aunt has grown older, she has developed diseases which seem directly related to her diet. Her doctor has warned her repeatedly to change her eating habits and cut down on her food intake. She has stubbornly refused to follow his orders, and now her gout is so bad she can barely walk. The pain is so intense that her foot feels as though it is on fire.

This aunt's situation is reminiscent of the incident in the Old Testament where Isaiah predicted that God would punish the king of Assyria and his warriors for the king's arrogance. Among other things, he was a little too self-satisfied and self-indulgent, a little too convinced that he, rather than God, knew the best way to impose order on life.

Many times, we get arrogant and self-indulgent about our diets, even in the face of growing medical evidence that there is a right way and a wrong way to eat. It has become quite obvious that there is a connection between good health and a good diet—evident that there is some strong relationship between food and physical well-being in the laws of nature which God has established. Yet we act as though we know more than both God and our medical experts. We freely ignore the fundamental principles of good nutrition, and as a result, we destroy our health.

The best time to go on a well-balanced diet and get down to your "fighting weight" is when you're still in relatively good health. If you don't, you may not be destroyed by the Assyrians in your well-fed state, but you can expect the principles of good nutrition and proper weight maintenance to begin to work against you.

Prayer: Dear God, I thank You for the good health I have been enjoying. Make me more aware of the damage I can do to my body by overeating or eating the wrong things. Help me keep myself as healthy as possible by eating properly.

Breakfast:
 1/2 cup Garden of Eden grapefruit drink:
  Blend 1/2 cup unsweetened grapefruit juice and one ice
  cube until light and chilled (48)
 1 scrambled egg (82)
 1 slice whole wheat toast, with 1/2 teaspoon margarine (79)
 1 cup skim milk (88)
 Coffee or tea, no cream or sugar

Lunch:
 3 1/2 ounces flounder, baked or broiled (202)
 1/2 cup mixed vegetables (58)
 1 fresh peach (38)
 1 cup skim milk (88)

Dinner:
 3 ounces chicken, light meat, baked with 1/2 pineapple
  slice (182)
 1/2 baked acorn squash (86)
 1 teaspoon margarine (35)
 * 1 Baked Apple (94)

Snack:
 Tea with lemon wedge

Remember: During the day, drink 8 8-ounce glasses of water.

Day 19

Ho! Everyone who thirsts,/Come to the waters;/And you who have no money,/Come, buy and eat./Yes, come, buy wine and milk/Without money and without price./Why do you spend money for what is not bread,/And your wages for what does not satisfy?/Listen diligently to Me, and eat what is good,/And let your soul delight itself in abundance (Is. 55:1–2).

Read Isaiah 55:1–7.

A woman I know has a high-powered job selling commercial space for radio stations. Her work requires that she do a good deal of traveling to visit clients, and by Friday she is often completely exhausted. Her biggest problem, though, is that she periodically goes on food binges: She'll eat an entire box of chocolate cookies and drink at least a quart of milk at one sitting. Then, she'll skip her regular dinner.

She admits to feeling anxious and lonely at such times, and she has feelings of emptiness she can't fill with food. From what I've observed and read, these feelings seem rather common among people who are binge eaters. What she can't seem to understand, even though many Christian friends have tried to explain it to her, is that mere food can't possibly supply the relief from her feelings of frustration and loneliness. Only God can satisfy the void that cries out for fulfillment within us.

God calls us through His Son Jesus to come and enjoy the spiritual feast that He has prepared for us, the Bread of Life that will always gratify our deepest needs and longings. We can't buy this food, no matter how rich we are. Yet His table is open to all who come with faith in their hearts and a sincere desire to know God better. These are the people He will fill with the succulent fruits of His Spirit.

Try examining your feelings the next time you feel an urge to stuff yourself. Are you anxious or lonely? Do you feel unloved? Instead of heading for your kitchen, go to a quiet place and pray to your heavenly Father, who loves you so much. He will comfort you in your distress and fill you with His love.

Prayer: Dear Lord, teach me to turn to You in the lonely moments of my life. When I'm hungry for something beyond my understanding, fill my entire being with Your holy presence. Bring greater meaning to my life.

Breakfast:
   1 cup apricot juice (122)
   1 toasted pumpernickel bagel (140)
   1 poached egg (80)
   1 cup skim milk (88)
   Coffee or tea, no cream or sugar

Lunch:
   3 ounces canned pink salmon (120)
   1/2 cup boiled spinach (66)
   1 cup baked mushrooms (20)
   1 teaspoon margarine (35)
   1 cup skim milk (88)

Dinner:
   1/2 broiled tarragon chicken breast (160) (Sprinkle tarragon lightly over chicken before broiling.)
   1/2 stalk broccoli (23)
   1/2 cup carrots (20)
   1/2 cup green beans (30)
   1/2 cup fruit juice (64)

Snack:
   1 cup plain, low-fat yogurt (142)
   1/2 cup blueberries (45)

Remember: During the day, drink 8 8-ounce glasses of water.

Day 20

Now to Him who is able to do exceedingly abundantly above all that we ask or think, according to the power that works in us, to Him be glory in the church by Christ Jesus throughout all ages, world without end. Amen (Eph. 3:20–21).

Read Ephesians 3:14–21.

We all have those times when the pressures of life seem to build up beyond what we are able to bear. One woman, Julia, experienced just such a stressful period during one Christmas season when various deadlines at work, in her church responsibilities, and with family get-togethers seemed to be coming to a head all at once.

In the face of such overwhelming pressures, Julia's usual response was to stop going to her exercise class, which she usually attended three times a week. She knew regular aerobic exercise was essential for her weight maintenance and also for her ability to feel relaxed and energetic. "But if anything has to go, it will have to be my workout," she said.

This time, however, she decided to ask God's assistance before she took any action, and, as a result, she was provided with help in some of the most unlikely places. On the last day she had planned to attend her exercise class, she mentioned to an unmarried friend that she was going to have to drop out of the program for a few weeks. Her friend immediately said, "Don't drop out—I'll give you a hand with some of your Christmas shopping and cooking. I'll even help you with the church party you're planning. What do you want me to do?"

This offer was amazing to Julia because her friend had never socialized with her, and as far as Julia knew, the woman wasn't even a churchgoer. Soon, others appeared, seemingly out of nowhere, to volunteer and take some of the burden off her shoulders. Also, as the pressures on her were relieved by helpful friends, she also had insights about ways she could perform her remaining duties more efficiently.

"The pressure was miraculously transformed into relaxation," she said. "Also, those who were helping me seemed to get more joy out of the holiday period by giving rather than receiving, and I certainly appreciated being on the receiving end that time!"

We are so foolish when we fail to ask for God's assistance. His power is abundant, and He is able to do far more for us than we can ever imagine. Ask now that God will help you overcome any obstacles you may be facing in your New You exercise and diet program. He is much more creative than we can ever be on our own.

Prayer: Forgive me, Lord, for all the time I've wasted worrying about my problems instead of asking You for help. Show me how I can become more disciplined and effective in my weight loss program.

Breakfast:
   1/2 cup orange juice (56)
   1 cup enriched whole grain cereal (112)
   1 cup skim milk (88)

Lunch:
   Seafood Supreme:
      3 1/2 ounces tuna, canned in water (127) on
      1 slice oatmeal bread (60), topped by
      1 ounce shredded Swiss cheese (100) and
      1/2 cup pineapple chunks (52)
   Coffee or tea, no cream or sugar

Dinner:
   3 ounces broiled veal cutlet (200)
   1 cup cooked green beans and cauliflower (40)
   1 small baked potato (76)
   1 teaspoon margarine (35)
   1 cup tossed salad, with tomato, lettuce, and cucumber (20)
   1 cup skim milk (88)

Snack:
   1/2 cup plain, low-fat yogurt (71)
   1/2 cup fresh strawberries (26)

Remember: During the day, drink 8 8-ounce glasses of water.

Day 21

If you abide in Me, and My words abide in you, you will ask what you desire, and it shall be done for you (John 15:7).

Read John 15:1–11.

Of all the wonderful passages in the Bible, this may be my favorite verse. The closer I am to the Lord, the more meaning these words have for me.

Several times since I've been a Christian I've been acutely aware I was drifting away from God. In one of those cases, I was deeply involved in decorating the CBN (Christian Broadcasting Network) Center. In fact, my devotional times had been at least partially supplanted by my obsession with color schemes and furniture moving. Even when I was praying or reading the Bible, I found that my mind was not really on God. Instead, fabrics, colors, and textures kept intruding on my thoughts, cutting me off from the Lord.

Finally, I stepped back for a moment and examined what was happening to me. It quickly became apparent that my priorities were out of order. When I am "abiding" with the Lord, when I'm truly close to Him, I know that His words soothe and guide me— even in my decorating. I began to focus on God during my devotional times and consciously pushed my color schemes and furniture arrangements out of my mind. The result was that I once again discovered the harmony in my life that only a God-first system of priorities can provide.

Interestingly enough, I found that the decorating began to flow. God was concerned about decorating the center too. He even "planned" some of the color schemes!

The same principle of putting God first applies to dieting. If we spend all our time worrying about grocery shopping, cooking, and calorie counting, He may get pushed out of the process altogether. When that happens, life's priorities get jumbled, as they did with me and my decorating. But if we put God first and trust Him to remodel our bodies *His* way, the entire dieting experience will be much more enjoyable and effective. We only need to ask Him to take charge of our weight concerns. Then, He'll step right in and order our minds as He shapes up our bodies.

Prayer: Dear Lord, help me achieve a balance in my life as well as in my diet. I thank You that You have explained the way to achieve this in Your written Word.

Breakfast:
* 1 cup Bird Seed Cereal (110)
  1 cup skim milk (88)
  1 slice medium pineapple (88)

Lunch:
  1 ounce natural cheese (107)
  1 slice whole wheat bread (61)
  1 cup salad: tomato, avocado, mushrooms, and lettuce (50)
  1 teaspoon Italian diet dressing (8)

Dinner:
* 1/2 Raspberry Chicken breast (160)
* 1/4 cup cooked Brown and Wild Rice (44)
* 1 Artichoke Bottom with Petite Pois (80)
* 1 cup Green Salad (20)
* 1/2 piece Meringue Elegante (134)
  1 small, plain roll (115)
  Coffee or tea, no cream or sugar

Snack:
  1/2 cup skim milk (44)

Remember: During the day, drink 8 8-ounce glasses of water.

Day 22

...to know the love of Christ which surpasses knowledge; that you may be filled with all the fullness of God (Eph. 3:19).

Read Ephesians 3:14–19.

Have you ever had to increase or decrease the size of a recipe at the last minute? For an inexperienced cook confronted with many more or many fewer guests than anticipated, this can be an intimidating experience. All the ingredients have to be changed in the exact proportions, or the end product won't taste right. In fact, it may be inedible.

A friend of mind learned some spiritual dimensions to this lesson when she was asked to help out at a church supper. She decided to bake some rolls by using her aunt's recipe, which had always been a family favorite. Just as she was ready to begin, she learned that an extra thirty people were expected, and she had to recalculate the quantities on a large scale.

For a moment, she was upset because the change in the quantities was confusing, and she was worried she wouldn't have enough ingredients. Then she asked God to help her, and a wave of relaxation swept over her as she realized that God, not she, had become the head baker. As for the rolls, they turned out beautifully, and there were plenty for everyone.

Since this experience, she tells me, she always prays before calculating measurements of ingredients for any dish. Also, she is much more aware of what foods should go into everything her family eats. Her knowledge of what is most healthy, what is most balanced, and what is most likely to put on less weight is remarkable. But perhaps, it's not so remarkable. After all, God has become an active partner in her food preparation, as well as in the other activities of her life.

Prayer: Dear Lord, I accept Your invitation to join in the feast of love that You offer to all of us. Create in me a thankful and loving spirit. Teach me how to be filled to the measure of Your fullness.

Breakfast:
   ¹/₂ cup orange juice (56)
* 1 cup Bird Seed Cereal (110)
   1 cup strawberries (52)
   ¹/₂ cup skim milk (44)

Lunch:
   3 ounces mostly lean pot roast (222)
   1 cup steamed carrots (40)
   ¹/₂ cup watermelon (32)
   1 cup skim milk (88)
* 1 cup Green Salad (20)
   Coffee or tea, no cream or sugar

Dinner:
* ¹/₂ Lemon Chicken breast (160)
* ¹/₂ cup cooked Brown and Wild Rice (44)
* 1 cup Ratatouille (50)
* 1 cup French Carrot Salad (48)
* ¹/₂ cup Red, White, and Blue Dessert (40)
   Coffee or tea, no cream or sugar

Snack:
   ¹/₂ cantaloupe (82)

Remember: During the day, drink 8 8-ounce glasses of water.

Day 23

Blessed be the God and Father of our Lord Jesus Christ, the Father of mercies and God of all comfort, who comforts us in all our tribulation, that we may be able to comfort those who are in any trouble, with the comfort with which we ourselves are comforted by God (2 Cor. 1:3–4).

Read 2 Corinthians 1:3–7.

After the church service had ended, mothers and fathers were picking up their children from the nursery. As one eager little four year old came bounding out of the door, his mother grabbed him by the coat and asked, "What did you learn in Sunday school today?"

The child thought for a moment and then proudly replied, "God is my quilt!"

"What?" the mother said, trying not to laugh.

"God is my quilt," he repeated.

Then the mother looked at the lesson paper the little boy was clutching in his hand, and she saw some words quoted from the Twenty-third Psalm: "Thy rod and thy staff, they comfort me." The little boy's response now became clear to her. He had thought of the comforter on his bed when the passage had been discussed, and he had just substituted the word *quilt* when telling his mother about God's role in the lesson.

The little boy obviously liked the idea of God as a quilt, probably because he recalled how warm and secure he felt at home when he snuggled down into his blankets at night. There's a desire within all of us at times to find a warm, safe, protected haven from the many problems of life. Sometimes, like the child, we may feel most insulated from our daily trials when we burrow down under our bedclothes at night.

Other times, we seek our protection, our comfort, in food. Yet God wants to comfort us, and He has provided His Holy Spirit as a constant presence in our lives. In fact, He has called the Spirit our Comforter. Our challenge is to learn better what it means to make God our "quilt."

Prayer: Dear Heavenly Father, You have not promised that my life will be free from all trouble. But You have promised to comfort me in difficult times. Make me more aware of the presence of Your Spirit, my ultimate Comforter, when problems arise.

Breakfast:
   ¹/₂ cup pineapple chunks (52)
   1 scrambled egg (82)
   1 corn muffin (120)
   1 teaspoon margarine (35)
   1 cup skim milk (88)

Lunch:
   ¹/₂ cup split pea soup (35)
   3 ounces ground beef patty (235)
   ¹/₂ cup boiled or steamed cabbage (22)
   1 cup skim milk (88)

Dinner:
   6-ounce glass tomato juice (35)
   3 ounces baked salmon (155)
   ¹/₂ cup boiled spinach and mushrooms (40), with
   1 teaspoon margarine (35)
   ¹/₂ cup plain, low-fat yogurt (71), over
   ¹/₂ sliced peach (19)

Snack:
   3 whole grain crackers (34)
   ¹/₂ ounce any cheese (53)

Remember: During the day, drink 8 8-ounce glasses of water.

Day 24

They shall eat the fruit of their own way,/And be filled to the full with their own fancies (Prov. 1:31).

Read Proverbs 1:29–33.

A friend came home from the doctor's office acting extremely disgruntled. She called to tell me she had high blood pressure and the doctor had told her not to use salt.

"There's not much point in eating if everything is going to be tasteless!" she said. "Do you think they *really* know if salt has any connection with high blood pressure?" she then asked hopefully.

I replied that everything I had heard indicated salt was a definite contributor to high blood pressure. I encouraged her to follow the doctor's advice. I also told her of several foods with high salt content, such as bacon and celery. Finally, I reminded her about how loved and needed she was and how important it was for her to take care of herself.

It's amazing to me, with the considerable knowledge we have of the relationship between diet and good health, that so many people are willing to ignore that knowledge. Instead, many continue to eat foods that are high in fat content, calories, salt, or chemicals. They say, "There's no sense in living if you can't enjoy yourself."

But of course, people have been headstrong and insisted on "eating the fruit of their own way" since Solomon's time. In the Bible, the prophets continually warned the people not to be "stiff-necked" or they would lose all they had. Yet they went right on about their business, living without God and the sources of wisdom He provided for them.

Let's not allow ourselves to be like that. Rebelling against clear facts just doesn't make sense. Indeed, this sort of rebellion usually makes some sort of personal disaster inevitable. Let's toss out the sour human fruits and misconceptions that are dragging us down and make the nourishing, uplifting fruits of the Spirit more of a reality in our lives.

Prayer: Lord, help me to become more teachable. Open me to the greater knowledge of others and to a greater understanding of Your wisdom. I pray that I may be willing to learn all my life.

Breakfast:
   ¹/₂ grapefruit (55)
   1 poached egg (80)
   1 slice whole wheat toast (61)
   1 teaspoon margarine (35)
   Coffee or tea, no cream or sugar

Lunch:
   3 ounces roast lamb (231)
   1 cup St. John's Salad (111):
   Recipe for 2 cups:
      1 diced medium apple (86)
      10 sprigs watercress (2)
      ¹/₂ cup raspberries (49)
      6 leaves of lettuce and carrot slivers (6)
      1 tablespoon sweet oil (35)
      1 tablespoon honey, dash of lemon juice, and paprika (35)
   1 cup skim milk (88)

Dinner:
   3 ounces broiled sole with lemon (150)
   ¹/₂ cup sweet corn (82)
   1 baked potato, 1-2¹/₂ inches in diameter (76)
   1 cup tossed salad: tomato and cucumbers (20)
   ¹/₂ cup skim milk (44)
* ¹/₄ cup Spanish Cream (76)

Snack:
   ¹/₄ cup gelatin/fruit (44)

Remember: During the day, drink 8 8-ounce glasses of water.

Day 25

From [Christ] the whole body, joined and knit together by what every joint supplies, according to the effective working by which every part does its share, causes growth of the body for the edifying of itself in love (Eph. 4:16).

Read Ephesians 4:13–16.

A friend of mine had polio when she was a young girl. Even though the disease stopped short of completely crippling her body, her legs were left weak and undeveloped. As a result, she lacked the freedom of movement and strength of many other girls her age. Most devastating of all, she began to believe she was inferior to her classmates. That feeling of inadequacy plagued her into adulthood. She refused to participate in any athletic activities and always chose to sit on the sidelines while everyone else played.

Then, a change came into her life. She joined a prayer-and-share group made up of young women from her church, and over a period of months she began to trust the advice and judgment she received. It became apparent the others were deeply interested in her emotional and spiritual growth, and she began to weigh carefully everything they said to her—though sometimes the advice was not easy to take.

At one of these sessions, she was somewhat disconcerted when one of the women said, "You know, I think God wants *each* of us to take better care of our bodies. And that means building up our strength and energy levels as much as we can, so that we can serve Him better."

My friend agreed that it might be important for people in really good health to try to develop their bodies more fully, but certainly that advice didn't apply to someone like her.

"Why not?" one of the other prayer-group members asked. "Granted, each of us may have a different potential. We all need to reach the maximum levels of our potential."

The handicapped woman was somewhat taken aback by this suggestion. Since she had come to respect and trust the other women, however, she began to ponder this point. Finally, she told the others, "Maybe you're right. I should do more to reach my physical potential, whatever it may be. What steps do you suggest I take?"

One of the other women immediately invited her to an exercise class, and with many reservations, my friend agreed to attend. "At first, it was terribly embarrassing," she says. "I could do very few of the exercises while the others in my class were so flexible and strong. I kept going, though, and very gradually, I began to see an improvement. Then one day, I realized I was actually *enjoying* exercising! Now, it's become such an important part of my life I could never give it up."

Here again, we see the "Law of Use," as my husband calls it, in action. That is, if we are willing to use what God has given us to the fullest, He will give us more and more.

When the apostle Paul uses the image of the human body to illustrate the structure of the church, he doesn't assume that each part of the body is equally strong or fulfills the same function as any other part. Instead, he stresses the strengthening of each body member to its full potential, so that the power of the whole will be maximized by the relative strengths of each part.

This analogy applies to us when we work toward our individual potentials. We should strengthen and streamline our physical beings just as we build up our spiritual and intellectual beings. In this way, we'll be able to exert our greatest potential power in the mission He has selected for each of us.

Prayer: Dear Lord, help me reach the physical potential You desire for my body. Give me more strength and energy so that I can serve You better.

Breakfast:
    ¹/₂ cup orange juice (56)
    1 cup bran cereal (140)
    1 cup skim milk (88)
    ¹/₂ cup strawberries (26)

Lunch:
  Tuna sandwich (open face) (223):
    3½ ounces tuna, canned in water (152)
    1 teaspoon mayonnaise (35)
    1 slice whole wheat bread (61)
  4 crisp radishes (7)
  Fresh blueberry yogurt:
    ½ cup fresh blueberries (45), mixed with
    8 ounces plain, low-fat yogurt (71)
  Coffee or tea, no cream or sugar

Dinner:
  2 filets of Sole Foo Yung (247), made with broiled sole
    covered by ¼ cup noodles, sprinkled with poppy seeds (50)
  1 teaspoon margarine (35)
  1 cup green beans (60)
  1 medium peach (38), with 1 tablespoon Cool Whip (18)
  Coffee or tea, no cream or sugar

Snack:
  1 cup skim milk (88)
  1 apple (86)

Remember: During the day, drink 8 8-ounce glasses of water.

Day 26

Stolen water is sweet,/And bread eaten in secret is pleasant./But he does not know that the dead are there (Prov. 9:17–18).

Read Proverbs 9:17–18.

A woman I know always kept candy in a dish in her living room. She believed, rightly or wrongly, that if sweets were always readily available in the home, her children would be less likely to grow up craving to eat large quantities of sugar. I don't know what the result was with her children, but the theory certainly broke down as far as her husband was concerned.

As he reached middle age, he developed high blood pressure and had to watch his diet closely. She changed her menus and her style of cooking to help him, but the candy dish still remained in the living room. One day, however, she suddenly became aware that it was emptying more rapidly than it ever had before.

She questioned her children, but they claimed innocence. Then one night she observed her husband get up from the dinner table, enter the living room, glance steathily around, and grab a handful of candy. My friend decided from that point on that in the interest of her husband's health, she would not buy any more candy.

We may smile at this man's sneaky actions and perhaps even feel a little superior to him. But how many of us sometimes behave as he did?

We may be ashamed to indulge ourselves in front of others. But when we are alone, we lose control. You might be by yourself in an empty house or up late at night, when the other family members have gone to bed. In those solitary moments, it's easy to change into a full-blown glutton. I've heard people say they dare not keep a bag of cookies or a cake in the house because they are afraid they'll eat the entire goody at one time.

The taste of "stolen goodies" may seem sweet at the time. But I know from personal experience that later I always feel disgusted with myself. In my weakest moments, I turn to God for help in controlling myself. I may rely on words like those in Philippians 4:8, which are contained in today's prayer, to focus my attention on more constructive things than unhealthy or unnecessary food.

Prayer: Dear Lord, fill my mind with "whatever things are true, whatever things are noble, whatever things are just, whatever things are pure, whatever things are lovely, whatever things are of good report." If anything is "praiseworthy," help me think about such things.

Breakfast:
   1 cup orange juice (112)
   1 slice toasted whole wheat bread (61)
   1 soft-cooked egg (80)
   Coffee or tea, no cream or sugar

Lunch:
   1 cup lentil soup (195)
   3 ounces steamed shrimp (110)
   1 cup raw cauliflower buds (28)
   Coffee or tea, no cream or sugar

Dinner:
   1/2 broiled chicken breast (160)
   1 cup boiled or steamed snap beans (60)
   1 boiled medium potato with parsley (90)
   1 large ear boiled corn (155)
   1/4 cantaloupe (41)
   Coffee or tea, no cream or sugar

Snack:
   1 dip diet ice cream (74)

Remember: During the day, drink 8 8-ounce glasses of water.

Day 27

...the church, which is His body, the fullness of Him who fills all in all (Eph. 1:22–23).

Read Ephesians 1:18–23.

"I always eat when I'm bored," Mark said. "When I have nothing to do, I head for the kitchen. First, I make myself a cup of coffee. Then, I start thinking about what I should have to go with it. I'm not even hungry—just restless."

This is a common experience for many of us. In fact, entire advertising campaigns for snack foods and soft drinks have been built around the feeling of being at loose ends and not knowing what to do with oneself. The answer in the ads is to "hang out" with some friends and the food that is being promoted.

Ultimately, eating may be a destructive way to fill your free time, especially if you have a tendency toward a weight problem. Joining in volunteer service projects or helping others in any way can be an excellent means to spend your "dead time" and also to divert your attention from yourself and the temporary satisfaction you may get from food or drink.

Christian work, in particular, offers so many ways to get our minds off ourselves and onto others. That's why I think today's devotional verse is so important: It says that Christ fills us in every way. And how do we find Him? Again, the passage indicates His fullness can be found in that concrete body of people known as the church.

When we invite Christ into our lives, we lose our feelings of restlessness, not just because of the sense of peace and security He provides, but also because He has work for us to do. I don't know any truly committed Christians who are not busy people. Jesus calls on us to use our talents to help others.

In serving Him, we may discover new talents and gifts we never knew we possessed. I have known people who have never worked with their hands but who find a new joy in physical labor when it is done for God. I have seen shy people blossom and step into the spotlight with ease when they are called upon by the Lord to lead in some endeavor for Him. I have seen selfish individuals learn a new respect for their fellowman and become warm, compassionate, and outgoing, though they were previously cold and aloof.

Yes, Christ will fill our lives if we permit Him to do so. The evidence lies all around us, and the opportunity to join His cause and the work of His church is ours if only we open our eyes to the possibilities.

Prayer: Lord, please fill my life with Your presence. Use me wherever You need me. Let me glorify You in everything that I do.

Breakfast:
    1 cup orange juice (112)
    1 buckwheat pancake (146)
    1 teaspoon honey (20)
    1 cup skim milk (88)

Lunch:
    2 ounces natural cheese (214), on
    1 slice pumpernickel bread (79)
*   1 cup Green Salad (20)
    1 cup fresh melon (52)

Dinner:
    3/4 cup black pea soup (139)
    1/2 average lobster (92)
    Prophet Daniel Salad (85):
        1/2 cup cantaloupe and watermelon balls (27)
        1/2 cup strawberries (26)
        5 green olives (28), all arranged over
        6 leaves of fresh, crisp lettuce (4)
    1/2 cup skim milk (44)

Snack 1:
Decaffeinated diet drink

Snack 2:
    1/2 cup skim milk (44)

Remember: During the day, drink 8 8-ounce glasses of water.

Day 28

Men ate angels' food;/He sent them food to the full (Ps. 78:25).

Read Psalm 78:23–29.

During our early days of walking with the Lord, Pat and I would often discuss the "bread of heaven" or "manna." It was a delicious topic because at that time, we frequently didn't have the price of a loaf of bread.

Although we had no weight problems then, we were never hungry and neither were our children. For one thing, the Lord made use of my knowledge of nutrition and the "basic four" food groups. Also, He introduced us to the mighty soybean. In fact, we began to refer to the soybean as our "manna" from heaven!

The Lord taught me how to use the soybean by helping me see that it could be substituted for the other types of beans suggested in my cookbooks. I also began to use it in place of ground beef in meat loaf, chili, and other dishes. We may not have liked everything we ate, but we were well-nourished and healthy. Instead of using our money for expensive meats, I could use it for milk, fruits and vegetables, and cereals. When it came to "love waffles," one of the items on today's breakfast menu, we did feel we were eating the "bread of angels"!

One lesson we can learn from all this in regard to weight control is that red meat is not necessary to a healthy diet. In many ways, it is harmful, for it is high in calories, fats, and cholesterol; we should learn to eat less of it.

Instead of steaks, roasts, or hamburgers every night, we need to think more in terms of beans, chicken, and fish. You'll notice I didn't include cheese in the acceptable list. Much of it is also high in fat and cholesterol! Cheese has been one of the hardest foods for me to stop eating. I find it to be habit-forming, like jelly beans and peanuts!

Prayer: Dear Lord, help me to seek Your will in the things that I eat. You created it all, and I know it is all good. But there are some things I should not eat. Reveal them to me and help me to refrain from them at all times. Thank You, Father, for Your guidance and direction.

Breakfast
>   6-ounce glass tomato juice (35)
> * 2 Love Waffles (180)
>   1/2 cup fresh strawberries (26)
>   1/4 cup plain, low-fat yogurt (35)
>   Coffee or tea, no cream or sugar

Lunch:
>   3 1/2 ounces tuna, canned in water (127)
>   1 slice whole wheat bread (61)
>   1 medium apple (86)
>   Decaffeinated coffee or soft drink

Dinner:
>   3 ounces broiled veal chops (200)
>   1 cup cooked zucchini (22)
>   1 baked potato, 1-2 1/2 inches in diameter (76)
>   1 teaspoon butter or margarine (35)
> * 1 cup Green Salad (20)
>   Coffee or tea, no cream or sugar

Snack:
>   1/2 cup skim milk (44)

Remember: During the day, drink 8 8-ounce glasses of water.

Day 29

I discipline my body and bring it into subjection, lest, when I have preached to others, I myself should become disqualified (1 Cor. 9:27).

Read 1 Corinthians 9:24–27.

A middle-aged acquaintance had tried some intermittent jogging in an effort to firm up some of his flabby muscles and to rediscover a measure of the energy of his youth. But he just couldn't seem to get himself to work out on a regular basis, and that frustrated him.

Then a friend quoted the old saying, "You are more likely to hit the target if you shoot for the moon." In the hope of hitting his target, which was to run regularly over at least medium distances for the rest of his life, he decided to "shoot for the moon." In short, he committed himself to run in the next local marathon.

"I never had any thought of coming close to winning," he explained. "The challenge was to run the same course as some of the best runners in our area and to finish."

This commitment required daily training on a much more strenuous level than he had known before. He stuck with it and even took a week of his vacation time just before the race so that he could concentrate fully on his effort.

He managed to finish in the middle of the pack, but the way he felt, he could easily have placed first. As he puts it, "The whole thing was well worth it because I learned what an exciting experience it is to build up your body to its maximum strength and then test it. Also, I started feeling alive and energetic in ways that I had never dreamed possible. Finally, and I think most important, I knew I could never return to undisciplined, irregular exercise. I didn't plan to run in any more marathons, but I did plan to keep my body in top shape."

I've never been interested in running, though both Pat and my oldest daughter jog, but I could understand this man's exhilaration. When I allow my calisthenic-and-walking routine to lapse, I know, somewhere deep inside myself, that things just aren't right.

Each of us is running to achieve an ultimate prize, which is eternal life with God. Our bodies are key factors in the race we are able to run. To stay in tip-top shape for the entire course of our lives, we must discipline both our bodies and our minds. A heavy, sluggish body will cause anyone to withdraw from new experiences and perhaps avoid taking on new responsibilities that can add excitement and inspiration to life.

Prayer: Dear Lord, help me achieve the capacity and endurance to enter into the mainstream of life. Help me run with the greatest power and energy. Make me aware You are always with me, from the very beginning to the very end.

Breakfast:
  1/2 medium grapefruit (55)
  1 soft-cooked egg (80)
  1 teaspoon butter or margarine (35)
  1 slice whole wheat bread (61)
  Coffee or tea, no cream or sugar

Lunch:
  2 stalks celery (14)
  3 ounces ground round lean beef (235)
  1 teaspoon mayonnaise (35)
  1 slice whole wheat bread (61)
  1 cup skim milk (88)

Dinner:
* 3 ounces Skewered Lamb (199)
  1 cup zucchini (25)
  1 baked potato, 1-2 1/2 inches in diameter (76), no butter or
    sour cream
* 1/4 cup Cucumber-Mint Salad with nuts (23)
* 4 ounces Spanish Cream with strawberries (130)
  Coffee or tea, no cream or sugar

Snack:
  1 cup lemonade (81)

Remember: During the day, drink 8 8-ounce glasses of water.

Day 30

We do not look at the things which are seen, but at the things which are not seen. For the things which are seen are temporary, but the things which are not seen are eternal (2 Cor. 4:18).

Read 2 Corinthians 4:16–18.

When I told an acquaintance, a man in his late forties, how youthful and fit he was looking, he laughed and said his present appearance was a relatively recent development in his life.

"One very hot day last summer, I caught an unexpected glimpse of myself in one of those full-length mirrors they use in stores. My suit jacket was off, and I saw more of myself than usual. The sight wasn't very encouraging."

He said his first thought was, "Who is that old guy?" Then, a split second later, he realized he was looking at himself!

"I didn't feel that old inside," he said. "So I decided to do something about my appearance and try to bring it more into line with my mental image of myself."

Sometimes, it takes a sudden shock like this to make us realize that we don't look the way we think we do. We can be totally unprepared for a reflection of ourselves in a large mirror, or for a candid snapshot that reveals that extra weight around the middle, or for a rear or side view of ourselves in a department store fitting room.

Instead of getting depressed, it's best to react as this man did: Realize that your present poor physical condition can be temporary. Fasten onto an improved image of yourself in your mind, and decide to make it a reality.

Some time ago, another friend was on a diet. Her mother sent her a picture taken when my friend weighed fifteen pounds less. Staring at that picture for a few minutes was enough to fix an ultimate weight-loss goal in her thoughts and motivate her to lose those extra pounds. One idea would be to post a picture like that near the scale or on the refrigerator door.

A positive mental image of yourself as an attractive and vital person can be the best starting point to embarking on a life-changing diet and exercise program. It can be a powerful weapon in forging the New You.

Prayer: Dear God, thank You for Your words, which assure me that what I now see need only be temporary. Grant me the will power not to become discouraged; give me the strength to continue in my struggle to lose weight and become fit.

Breakfast:
* 1 cup Bird Seed Cereal (110)
  1 cup skim milk (88)
  1 cup strawberries (55)
  Coffee or tea, no cream or sugar

Lunch:
6-ounce glass tomato juice (35)
3 ounces very lean hamburger (238)
Lettuce and slice of tomato (20)
2 slices dill pickle (30)
Decaffeinated coffee or soft drink

Dinner:
1 halibut filet (214)
2 stalks broccoli (94)
1 slice cheddar cheese (139)
1 cup spinach salad with mushrooms and lemon juice (20)
Coffee or tea, no cream or sugar

Snack:
1 medium apple (86)

Remember: During the day, drink 8 8-ounce glasses of water.

Day 31

Do you not know that your body is the temple of the
Holy Spirit who is in you, whom you have from God,
and you are not your own? (1 Cor. 6:19).

Read 1 Corinthians 6:12–20.

On a trip to Europe a few years ago, I was overwhelmed by
the towering, ethereal arches of the cathedrals in Italy. It amazed
me that man has been able to create such magnificent places of
worship.

The ceilings, if they can even be called ceilings, seem to reach
up to the sky. Sometimes, as with the sky itself, it's impossible to
tell where the uppermost reaches of the cathedrals actually end.
Moreover, the beautiful, intricate stained glass casts its multicol-
ored images off the columns and walls so that it appears that wor-
shipers have entered the inside of a rainbow.

When you enter one of these magnificent structures, your
speech automatically lowers to a whisper. No other volume of
voice fits into the architecturally induced atmosphere of adoration
and praise.

The designers of these cathedrals knew something of the
Spirit that would move through these hallowed halls. They perhaps
came as close as humanly possible to creating an appropriate physical space that would evoke an attitude of prayer and worship.

Yet when I think of what God has done in creating the human
body, the effect is even more marvelous and miraculous. The
bricks and mortar of our bodies, the cells and bones and muscles
that make up our physical beings, are a much more miraculous ca-
thedral than human hands could ever fashion. What an incredible
edifice to house something greater than man himself—namely, the
Spirit of God.

And what a responsibility each of us has as a "sexton" of his
tremendous temple. To use this body in the wrong way, to neglect
its muscle tone, to fill it full of excessive or harmful food is a sacri-
lege of sorts, if we really believe it is the temple of God's Spirit. We
must do our best to maintain the physical nature that has been entrusted to us.

Prayer: Thank You, God, for making me the earthly steward of my body. Help me to take my responsibility seriously, and show me exactly what I can do to make the best use of my physical being in Your service.

Breakfast:
   ¹/₂ cup bran cereal (70)
   1 cup skim milk (88)
   4 ounces orange juice (56)
   Coffee or tea, no cream or sugar

Lunch:
   Chef's salad, with vinegar (351):
      ¹/₄ head lettuce (18)
 *   1 serving Cucumber-Mint Salad (23)
      1 tomato (28)
      6 slices of coldcuts (200)
      1 hard-boiled egg (82)
   1 cup skim milk (88)

Dinner:
   ¹/₂ broiled tarragon chicken breast (160) (Sprinkle chicken
      lightly with tarragon before broiling.)
 *   ¹/₂ cup cooked Brown and Wild Rice (88)
   ¹/₂ cup snap beans (30)
   6 cherries (30)
   Coffee or tea, no cream or sugar

Snack:
   1 cup skim milk (88)

Remember: During the day, drink 8 8-ounce glasses of water.

Day 32

For bodily exercise profits a little, but godliness is profitable for all things, having promise of the life that now is and of that which is to come (1 Tim. 4:8).

Read 1 Timothy 4:6–9.

I heard of a man in terrible physical condition. As is often the case, his image of himself and his level of self-confidence were as low as the state of his health.

Then he discovered running. He became involved in amateur racing, too, including the marathon circuit. His physical condition improved markedly, and so did his view of himself. He became more adept at dealing with people in his business and social affairs.

The long hours of training, an hour and a half or two hours a day, began to wear on some of his other responsibilities, especially on his family life. Finally, his wife, a "marathon widow," decided she had had enough. She asked him for a separation agreement, and eventually they got a divorce.

In this man's case, physical training was certainly of some value. But without the integrating power of a faith in God, a faith that puts Jesus Christ first, the true value of exercise could never be realized. He had made an idol of his training.

Contrary to what some deeply religious people think, a mature spirituality doesn't presuppose a disregard of the body. Christian maturity does involve an integration of mind, body, and soul under God our Father. There must be a setting of priorities ordained by the Lord that we must follow. In other words, God—not our aerobic conditioning or our image of a beautiful body—must become the primary standard that orders the rest of our lives.

Prayer: Lord, help me to make good nutrition and regular exercise a part of my life. At the same time, show me how to fit these physical considerations into the new creation I am becoming in You.

Breakfast:
  1/2 fresh grapefruit (55)
  1 toasted whole wheat English muffin (130)
  1 poached egg (80)
  1/2 cup skim milk (44)

Lunch:
  1/2 cup plain, low-fat yogurt, sprinkling of blueberries (85)
  2 stalks broccoli (94)
  1 cup skim milk (88)

Dinner:
  3 1/2 ounces broiled cod (170)
* 1/4 cup cooked Brown and Wild Rice (44)
* 1/2 cup Apple Walnut Salad (71), on
  6 crisp lettuce leaves (4)
* 1/2 cup Hot Spiced Fruit (61)
  Coffee or tea, no cream or sugar

Snack:
  1/2 cup skim milk (44)
  22 medium seedless grapes (69)

Remember: During the day, drink 8 8-ounce glasses of water.

Day 33

For every creature of God is good, and nothing is to be refused if it is received with thanksgiving (1 Tim. 4:4).

Read 1 Timothy 4:1–5.

Jack started on several diet programs and immediately quit them because he considered most of the food he was required to eat tasteless or uninteresting. In the New You diet, I've tried to correct this problem by including the most elegant low-calorie dishes I know, dishes Pat and I have found to be quite suitable for entertaining guests, as well as for losing excess weight.

Jack didn't know about the New You diet, and also he was a big meat eater; he couldn't really get interested in vegetables. He was an intelligent person, however, and was able to get enthusiastic about new fields of knowledge that caught his fancy.

At some point, perhaps during his fourth or fifth attempt at weight loss, his wife hit upon a plan that fit his personality. She referred him to the above verse and told him that he should make good nutrition a personal project or hobby, just as he did his woodworking and athletic activities.

"Look, just assume that verse in the Bible is correct—that all the food you eat on a healthy diet is really good for you," she said. "Then, do two things: Number one, get some books on nutrition and learn more about what this food does for you inside your body. And number two, get some cookbooks and figure out ways that you and I can prepare the food to make it taste great."

The challenge of becoming a food expert fascinated Jack. He knew nothing about nutrition or about cooking; he embarked on a crash program to learn more than any of his friends and relatives about these subjects. The result was that in just a few weeks, he became the "food expert" in whatever family or social gathering he attended. The foods he had previously thought were uninteresting became some of his favorites because he knew more about how they were helping him increase his energy levels, balance out the nutrients in his system, and lose weight. Many more foods had become "good" in Jack's way of thinking because he had simply taken time to learn more about them.

Prayer: Lord, help me find a way to love the foods I should eat. Help me to understand good nutrition and the proper quantities I am to consume. Show me how essential they are to the health of the body You have given me.

Breakfast:
* * 1 cup Bird Seed Cereal (110)
  1 cup skim milk (88)
  1/2 cup pineapple chunks (52)
  1 slice whole wheat toast (61)

Lunch:
  1/2 cup grapefruit juice (48)
  1/2 ounce natural cheese on 1 slice cracked wheat bread (111)
  1 cup Avocado Special: Tomato, avocado, mushrooms, lettuce, and diet dressing (50)

Dinner:
* * 1/2 Raspberry Chicken breast (160)
* * 1/4 cup cooked Brown and Wild Rice (44)
  1/2 cup peas (40)
* * 1 cup Green Salad (20)
  1 hard roll (50)
* * 1/4 piece Meringue Elegante (134)

Snack:
  1/2 cup plain, low-fat yogurt (71)
  1 orange (66)

Remember: During the day, drink 8 8-ounce glasses of water.

Day 34

If any of those who do not believe invites you to dinner,
and you desire to go, eat whatever is set before you, asking no question for conscience' sake (1 Cor. 10:27).

Read 1 Corinthians 10:27–33.

Sometimes it's all too easy to get self-righteous about a diet or
exercise program, especially in the early, highly enthusiastic
phases. A young man named Mike discovered aerobic exercise and
a low-fat diet at the same time, and the result was almost too much
for his sister, whom he visited just after he started his program.

When he sat down for his first meal at her home, she placed
before him one of his favorite dishes, a cheese and beef casserole
which she had painstakingly prepared. She fully expected him to
shovel half the casserole onto his plate. Consequently, she had included a larger amount than she usually prepared for her own family.

But Mike turned up his nose and said, "I'm sorry, but I'm not
allowed to eat this—my new diet, you know. I think I'll just stick to
the salad."

Then he proceeded to give his sister and her husband a lec-
ture on the basics of good nutrition which he had picked up during
the previous week, when he had started his new regimen.

Within a couple of months, Mike had modified this diet to in-
corporate some of his old, favorite foods, with some adjustments
in light of his increasing knowledge about good nutrition. It took
much longer to repair his relationship with his sister.

She had been offended, and rightly so, by his high-handed,
insensitive criticism of the meal she had so lovingly prepared for
him. It was possible after a while for her to say, "Oh, well, that was
just Mike!" But the hurt he had inflicted could have been avoided if
he had just scraped off some of the cheese, taken a small portion,
and kept his mouth closed.

Prayer: Dear God, give me the sensitivity to strike a balance
between a healthy diet and a healthy attitude about the knowledge
of good nutrition that I'm gaining. Help me to put people above
food.

Breakfast:
* 1 medium Love Waffle (90)
  1/2 cup plain, low-fat yogurt (62)
  1/2 cup red raspberries (41)
  4 ounces orange juice (55)
  Coffee or tea, no cream or sugar

Lunch:
  3 ounces veal and mushrooms (210)
  Chef's salad, with vinegar:
    1/4 head lettuce (18)
* 1/4 cup Cucumber-Mint Salad (11)
    1 tomato (28)
  1 cup skim milk (88)

Dinner:
  3 1/2 ounces broiled halibut (182)
  1 cup cooked carrots (40)
  1/4 cup scalloped potatoes, without cheese (94)
* 1/2 piece Meringue Elegante (134)
  Coffee or tea, no cream or sugar

Snack:
  1 slice pineapple (88)
  1 cup strawberries (52)

Remember: During the day, drink 8 8-ounce glasses of water.

Day 35

Therefore, my brethren, when you come together to eat,
wait for one another (1 Cor. 11:33).

Read 1 Corinthians 11:27–34.

In one family, the members have fallen into the habit of rarely sitting down at the table and eating the evening meal together. Instead, the son, consumed with his athletic interests, rushes in and gets some food on the run. Then he rushes out again to play another round of ball. The daughter makes only a quick "pit stop" to bolt down a piece of chicken or beef between social activities. The husband, a hard-driving businessman, gets home at odd hours, sometimes as late as ten or eleven o'clock.

The wife, usually left to eat alone, piles her plate full of food and plops down in front of the TV to watch the evening news. She eats quickly and often goes back for seconds or thirds, without thinking seriously about what she's doing. As a result, she's begun to overeat and is already twenty pounds overweight.

The main problem this woman faces with her weight is not that she is eating out of frustration. Rather, because of her family's schedule, all the safeguards against excessive food consumption have been knocked out from under her. As a result, she's become vulnerable to some of the most insidious pressures to overeat.

For one thing, the television set has taken the place of family conversation. Among diet experts television has become notorious for practically hypnotizing those who are eating in front of it. Before a person becomes aware, he may consume far more food than he would otherwise. Also, the social restraints on eating too quickly, which often exist in a group setting, including the pressure to pay closer attention to table manners, don't apply.

Researchers have discovered that it takes about twenty minutes from the time you begin to eat for your brain to start registering whether you're eating too much. As this woman shovels in the food during her TV programs, she gets far too much into her stomach before her mental warning signals begin to operate.

Obviously, Paul was concerned about issues that went far beyond considerations of diet when he wrote the words in today's Bible passage. But he was also interested in the development of the *whole* man and woman. It's not surprising that his warning to "wait for one another" has important weight loss implications as well.

Prayer: Lord, help me to slow my life and reduce the pressures I live under each day. Show me how to enjoy my family, friends, and food at a more reasonable pace.

Breakfast:
    ¹/₂ cup apple juice (58)
    1 scrambled egg (82)
    1 slice whole wheat bread (61)
    Coffee or tea, no cream or sugar

Lunch:
    ¹/₂ cup grapefruit and mandarin orange sections (40)
    1 slice avocado pear (80), sprinkled with
    1 tablespoon coconut and nuts (44)
    1 cup skim milk (88)
    3 ounce lean veal cutlet (200)
*   ¹/₄ cup cooked Brown and Wild Rice (44)
    Coffee or tea, no cream or sugar

Dinner:
*   ¹/₂ cup Asparagus Consommé (70)
    3¹/₂ ounces baked flounder (200)
    1 cup zucchini (33)
    1 plum (22)
*   1 slice Surprise Bread (119)

Snack:
    1 peach (38)
    ¹/₄ cup cranberries (13)

Remember: During the day, drink 8 8-ounces glasses of water.

Day 36

Then as he lay and slept under a broom tree, suddenly
an angel touched him, and said to him, "Arise and eat"
(1 Kin. 19:5).

Read 1 Kings 19:4–8.

In this passage from the Old Testament, Elijah, under the guidance of God, has just won a major confrontation with the prophets
of the false god Baal on Mount Carmel. But then, he has a "let-
down" after his great victory and gets so depressed that he actually
asks God to take his life.

How could such a great man of God have such a negative attitude, especially after he has just witnessed the power of the Divine
so dramatically in his life?

It seems fairly clear to me from the entire reading today that
Elijah was suffering in large part from fatigue and a lack of food. All
he needed was to get some sleep and some food from the angel,
and then he was his spry old self once again.

Many times, you may also start feeling "down" even though
you just can't seem to put your finger on what the problem is.
Everything may be going right with your family and work. In fact,
you have so much to be thankful for, it seems ludicrous to be unhappy. Yet you *are* unhappy.

People who seem to be the most fortunate among us sometimes also seem to be the unhappiest. To solve their problems, they
may begin to search for deep psychological reasons for their discomfort and may even consider seeking medical help when, actually, their only problem may be a lack of adequate sleep or good
nutrition.

If you're feeling a little low, try getting an extra couple of
hours sleep tonight. Check your eating habits to see if you're eating
a balanced diet, including sufficient amounts of complex carbohydrates, high energy foods like fruits and vegetables. Also, for children who get a little grouchy an hour or so before dinner, or adults
who come in tired after a long day at work, a snack of fruit or vegetables around 5:00 P.M. may be just the thing.

Like Elijah, you may find there is a physical basis to your emotional and even your spiritual problems.

Prayer: Lord, put me in touch with my feelings. Give me the ability to analyze my emotions so that I can identify negative thoughts and attitudes.

Breakfast:
   ¹/₂ cup orange juice (56)
   1 hard-boiled egg (82)
   1 slice whole wheat toast (61)
   ¹/₂ grapefruit broiled with Tab (55)
   Coffee or tea, no cream or sugar

Lunch:
   3 ounces chuck veal (200)
   1 cup steamed eggplant (38)
   1 cup broiled mushrooms (20)
   1 cup cooked tomatoes (51)
   Coffee or tea, no cream or sugar

Dinner:
   6-ounce glass tomato juice (35)
   1 cup summer squash (29)
   1 cup tossed salad (20)
 * 3 ounces Swedish Meatballs (318)
      (Note: This dish should usually be eaten as part of an
      "open house" menu. See chapter 5.)
 * ¹/₂ piece Meringue Elegante (134)

Snack:
   ¹/₂ cup grapefruit juice (48)

Remember: During the day, drink 8 8-ounce glasses of water.

Day 37

This shall be a perpetual statute throughout your genera-
tions in all your dwellings: you shall eat neither fat nor
blood (Lev. 3:17).

Read Leviticus 3:12–17.

It's reassuring to me to see how many of the rules and principles laid down in the Old Testament are echoed in modern findings
in science and medicine.

Take today's verse, for example. The rule about no fat or
blood obviously went far beyond any nutritional considerations:
God wanted His people to learn to obey Him without question,
even when they might not understand exactly why He was asking
them to do something.

I can't help feeling that perhaps one of the reasons He laid
down this rule in His law was that He wanted to encourage good
food habits. Perhaps He knew the Israelites of that time wouldn't
comprehend the dangers of ingesting too much cholesterol or saturated fat. Having made all things in the universe, He knows best
what is good for us and what isn't, even if we don't.

I know God must have had many other things in mind other
than good nutrition when He posited this principle. Yet today, our
scientists are finding our high rate of coronary heart disease can be
traced to too much cholesterol in animal meats and the failure of
our systems to process and clean out excessive saturated fats. It
would seem that this divine guideline, laid down so long ago,
might have been designed to provide us with healthy bodies as
well as obedient and trusting spirits.

Prayer: Lord, teach me to trust You, even when I can't understand Your will or plan for my life. Help me to walk by faith, not by
sight.

Breakfast:
    1 cup unsweetened bran cereal (140), with
    1 banana (100)
    3/4 cup skim milk (66)
    Coffee or tea, no cream or sugar

Lunch:
   Tuna salad sandwich (open face) (292):
      3½ ounces tuna, canned in water (127), mixed with
      2 teaspoons mayonnaise (100)
      6 lettuce leaves (4)
      1 slice whole wheat bread (61)
   1 slice honeydew melon (61)
   Coffee or tea, no cream or sugar

Dinner:
* 1 serving, Wild Rice Casserole (150)
* ½ cup Ratatouille (50)
* 1 cup French Carrot Salad (40)
   1 stalk broccoli (47)
* 1 slice Surprise Bread (119)
   Coffee or tea, no cream or sugar

Snack:
   1 medium apple (86)

Remember: During the day, drink 8 8-ounce glasses of water.

Day 38

It is vain for you to rise up early,/To stay up late,/To eat the bread of sorrows;/For so He gives His beloved sleep (Ps. 127:2).

Read Psalm 127.

Often I've heard hard-driving businessmen and women describe the late hours they keep as they try to meet deadlines. One man I know has even calculated how much time he "loses" each day while he sleeps. He's attempted gradually to cut back on his time in bed in order to leave more time for work!

There's a point of diminishing returns in this game. Creativity, relaxation, and the very joy of life may disappear if we try to cram too many activities into time that God has ordained for our rest.

I've found that when I trust Him, God actually works during my sleep to make things easier for me when I wake up to face my tasks the next day. If I've had enough rest, I have insights the next day that were impossible for me in the midst of the fatigue the day before.

If you feel your work getting out of control and encroaching on other areas of your life, including those all-important times of rest and sleep, make this verse your slogan. Believe that God will deliver on His promise to give you sleep *and* successful achievement, and He'll do just that.

Prayer: Lord, help me to strike the right balance in my life between work and rest, between intense activity and sound sleep.

Breakfast:
    1 cup bran cereal (140)
    $^1/_2$ cup fresh blueberries (45)
    1 cup skim milk (88)

Lunch:
    $^1/_2$ cup papaya juice (60)
    Turkey sandwich (230):
        1 slice cracked wheat bread (60)

3¹/₂ ounces sliced turkey, white meat (176)
1 cup salad: green beans, kidney beans, dash of vinegar (30)
Coffee or tea, no cream or sugar

Dinner:
　5 ounces calf liver (180) sautéed in
　1 teaspoon margarine (35)
　1 ear corn (100)
　1 cup tossed salad: lettuce and spinach (20), with
　1 teaspoon olive oil (35)
　¹/₂ cup tangerine juice (54)

Snack:
　¹/₄ avocado, with 1 teaspoon mayonnaise (107)

Remember: During the day, drink 8 8-ounce glasses of water.

Proverbial Meal Planning

　Now, let's embark on a brief excursion through the Proverbs. These words from Solomon and other Hebrew wise men give us some of the best insights into the spiritual implications of good nutrition.

Day 39

A companion of gluttons shames his father (Prov. 28:7).

Read Proverbs 28:1–7.

An extremely fat woman, Marge, was a member of the board of a community organization. During the organization's weekly meetings, she would pile upon her plate mountains of goodies that were put out as snacks.

Behind her back, the other members shook their heads at her behavior and criticized her lack of self-restraint. Yet there was an element of hyprocrisy in their criticisms: several of her colleagues tended to eat more sweets at these meetings than they did otherwise, and soon they found they were putting on extra weight, too.

Then, one of the more perceptive and sensitive members, who had also been participating in the mini-food orgies, realized what was happening. She immediately brought up her concerns to some of the others: "As we all know, Marge has a weight problem. But let's face it: So do we! Instead of criticizing her, let's decide what we can all do about the situation."

Reluctantly, the others admitted she had a point, and they formulated a strategy to help Marge as well as themselves. First, they decided to put out fewer fattening snacks at these meetings and to substitute "vegies" and fruits for pastries and cheese. Next, for their own good and as an example to Marge, they resolved to help one another stay away from overindulging in the snacks that were offered. Finally, instead of talking about Marge behind her back, they tried to communicate with her and help her get to the root of her weight problem.

In other words, these women stopped being companions who participated in Marge's excesses and became constructive companions who helped her, as well as themselves. This same principle could be applied to friends who have drinking problems.

Prayer: Lord, help me to approach with humility others who have weight problems. Enable me to remember that pride has no place in my New You diet program.

Breakfast:
* ¹/₂ cup Bird Seed Cereal (55)
  1 cup skim milk (88)
  1 cup fresh strawberries (52)

Lunch:
  ¹/₂ broiled tarragon chicken breast (160) (Sprinkle
    tarragon lightly over chicken before broiling.)
* ¹/₄ cup cooked Brown and Wild Rice (44)
  1 cup tossed salad with dash of vinegar (20)
  1 large sliced tomato (44)
  1 cup skim milk (88)

Dinner:
  1 chopped cucumber (45)
  3¹/₂ ounces baked flounder (200)
  1 cup cooked carrots (40)
  1 cup skim milk (88)
* 1 cup Green Salad (20)

Snack:
  2 small slices pineapple (82)
  1 cup yogurt with raisins (162)

Remember: During the day, drink 8 8-ounce glasses of water.

Day 40

Do not love sleep, lest you come to poverty;/Open your eyes, and you will be satisfied with bread (Prov. 20:13).

Read Proverbs 20:1–13.

This verse acts as an interesting counterpoint to Psalm 127:2, which we considered recently. In the psalm, we were told to get enough sleep. Here, we are brought into proper balance. You can also sleep too much, Solomon says.

Most of us have a tendency to be too sedentary, especially as we get older. It's much easier to sit and let others do for us, instead of doing for ourselves. We should remain active if we hope to continue to achieve important goals in life. Physical activity is also necessary if we hope to burn up the calories that threaten to accumulate on our bodies as the years go by.

One woman does exactly what Solomon is warning against. She dozes on her coffee breaks; she dozes before the television set when she gets home at night; and she dozes for hours on end on the weekends. The result: She has put on about five extra pounds for each of the past five years, and now she is far above her ideal weight.

Activity brings excitement into our lives. Energy breeds energy. Exercise acts as a crucial element in weight control. God has created us not only to rest and sleep in sufficient amounts but also to get out into the world and pursue an active and vigorous life.

Prayer: Thank You, Lord, for giving me mobility. Help me to find new ways to channel my energies in Your service.

Breakfast:
    1 cup bran cereal (140)
    1 cup skim milk (88)
    1 cup orange juice (112)
    Coffee or tea, no cream or sugar

Lunch:
  3½ ounces broiled halibut (182)
  1 cup broccoli (94)
  ½ cup cooked rice (111)
  1 cup skim milk (88)

Dinner:
  ½ broiled chicken breast, no skin or fat (160)
  1 cup asparagus (52)
  1 baked potato, 1-2½ inches in diameter (76), no butter or
    sour cream
  6 leaves lettuce (4)
  1 medium raw tomato (33)
  1 tablespoon diet dressing (8)
  22 medium seedless grapes (69)
  Coffee or tea, no cream or sugar

Snack:
  1 cup unsweetened fresh fruit cocktail (91)

Remember: During the day, drink 8 8-ounce glasses of water.

Day 41

Have you found honey?/Eat only as much as you need,/
Lest you be filled with it and vomit (Prov. 25:16).

Read Proverbs 25:15–20.

This verse doesn't present a very pretty picture, does it? Yet
how many of us sit down with a box of cookies or a bag of jelly
beans and consume the entire thing at one sitting? I know I have. I
have a ferocious sweet tooth when I fail to control it.

Often after indulging in one of these binges, you feel nau-
seous. I'm not sure how much of this feeling is physical or how
much is emotional. In my case, I get just as sick at myself and my
lack of control as I do with the act of filling my stomach with junk
food!

God has created sweets for our enjoyment. Like anything else,
we can get too much of a good thing. Our entire lives as successful
dieters must be devoted, at least in part, to trying to find the proper
balance between the way God wants us to eat and act, and the way
we want to act in order to satisfy our own wishes and desires.

Prayer: Lord, thank You for making so many wonderful, tasty
things available for me. Give me the wisdom to know what to eat
and the discipline to consume just the right amounts.

Breakfast:
   ¹/₄ wedge honeydew melon (98)
   ¹/₂ cup bran cereal (70)
   1 cup skim milk (88)
   Coffee or tea, no cream or sugar

Lunch:
   3 ounces ground lean beef (235)
   1 slice packaged cheddar cheese (52)
   8 spears asparagus (24)
   3 leaves lettuce (2)
   1 medium tomato (33)
   1 teaspoon diet dressing (18)

Dinner:
   3 ounces steamed shrimp (110)
   1 cup eggplant (50)
   1 cup cooked carrots (40)
   1/2 cup scalloped potatoes (122), no cheese
 * 1/2 cup Green Salad (10)

Snack:
   1/2 cup fresh pineapple chunks (52)
   1/2 cup fresh strawberries (26)

Remember: During the day, drink 8 8-ounce glasses of water.

Day 42

"Eat and drink!" he says to you,/But his heart is not with you (Prov. 23:7).

Read Proverbs 23:6–8.

Meals are meant to be periods of sharing and fellowship, not times of tension and stress.

While you're in the first stages of the New You diet program, I recommend that you try to eat most of your meals in the presence of those who are pleasant and supportive of your goals. As far as possible, choose companions whose hearts are in your objectives.

Don't put yourself in difficult situations when you first get started. Avoid those who actively try to get you off your diet. Also, avoid those who are not so obvious, people who make fun or who bring tension into relationships and conversations. When you have developed solid nutritional habits, you'll be better able to withstand these pressures.

Distractions and frustrations are among the most devastating enemies of an effective weight-loss program.

Prayer: Lord, I pray for those who are insensitive to those of us who need to lose weight. Help me love them. At the same time, give me the means to escape the temptations they put in my path.

Breakfast:
   1 cup fresh grapefruit sections (60)
   1/2 cup hot oatmeal (74)
   1 cup skim milk (88)

Lunch:
   1/2 cup fruit special: pineapple, avocado, and strawberries (90)
   1/2 cup plain, low-fat yogurt (71)
   2 1/2 ounces boiled cornbeef (263)
   1/2 cup steamed cabbage (16)
* 1/4 cup cooked Brown and Wild Rice (44)

Dinner:

  3 ounces sirloin steak (260)
  2 broccoli stalks, steamed (58)
  1 baked potato, 1-2½ inches in diameter (76), no butter
    or sour cream
  ¾ cup skim milk (66)

Snack:

  1 cup fresh strawberries (52)

Remember: During the day, drink 8 8-ounce glasses of water.

Day 43

Bread gained by deceit is sweet to a man,/But afterward his mouth will be filled with gravel (Prov. 20:17).

Read Proverbs 20:17–24.

A young man named Joe began working at a new job where he had access to an expense account. One of the first bits of advice he got from two other employees on his level went like this: "You know, the expense account here is really regarded as part of your compensation. You're expected to put in for at least $30-35 a week, whether you incur any expenses or not. Just be sure you put in for it; because if you don't, you'll stick out and you may get into trouble."

Joe knew what they were really saying was, "If you fail to put in for those expenses, you'll get *us* into trouble."

Still, the temptation was tantalizing. Without doing any extra work, he could get an additional $1,500 or more a year tax-free. All he had to do was just merge into the crowd that was padding expenses. For several days, he brooded about this issue; he had little to say when his family gathered at mealtimes. In fact, when he did talk, it was usually to snap at one of his children or his wife.

His wife knew something was bothering him. At her urging, they finally talked it out. With her distance from the situation—and her inherent honesty—she knew Joe should refuse to go along with his colleagues. She showed him the above verse, and Joe knew immediately those words were meant for him.

In a very real sense, his "mouth had been full of gravel" at mealtimes until he settled on a more honest approach to his work. So it is for all of us: The way we conduct every aspect of our lives is intimately linked to the way we approach and enjoy our food.

Prayer: Dear God, help me become more spiritually mature. Show me how I can deepen my relationship with You in every dimension of my life.

Breakfast:
    1 cup orange juice (112)
*   Omelet (one egg), with assorted vegetable toppings (92)
    Coffee or tea, no cream or sugar

Lunch:
    3¹/₂ ounces broiled cod (170)
    ¹/₂ cup steamed broccoli (30)
    ¹/₂ cup summer squash (14)
    1 cup skim milk (88)
*   1 cup Minted Fresh Fruit (84)

Dinner:
    3 ounces ground lean beef (235)
    1 boiled fresh ear of corn (70)
*   ¹/₂ cup Cucumber-Mint Salad (23)
*   ¹/₄ cup Spanish Cream (76)
    1 cup skim milk (88)
    Coffee or tea, no cream or sugar

Snack:
    1 medium apple (86)

Remember: During the day, drink 8 8-ounce glasses of water.

Day 44

The sluggard will not plow because of winter;/Therefore he will beg during the harvest/And have nothing (Prov. 20:4).

Read Proverbs 20:1–5.

It's important to have a weight-loss goal. It's also important to settle on a sound, effective program to achieve that goal. Most important of all, you must embark on a daily routine of proper eating and healthy exercise. Otherwise, you'll never bridge the gap between your choice of dieting and the ultimate goal you want to achieve.

I think today's verse admirably sums up this point. Losing weight is a lot like bringing in a harvest. It's necessary to decide on what crops you want to grow and how you're going to raise them. Still, all this planning and goal setting will be useless without putting your shoulder to the plow, day by day, until the fields have been put in shape and the seeds sown.

Thinking about growing food doesn't bring it to market or put it on the table. Similarly, merely thinking about weight loss doesn't result in the removal of those pounds.

Prayer: Lord, help me to become a doer rather than just a dreamer. Give me the perseverance to chip away at those calories each day for the next few weeks until I reach my weight-loss goal.

Breakfast:
   1/2 grapefruit (55)
   1/2 cup hot Ralston (74)
   1 cup skim milk (88)

Lunch:
   3 ounces broiled chuck roast (279)
   1 steamed broccoli stalk (47)
   1 small bread stick (10)
   1 fresh peach (38)
   1/2 cup skim milk (44)

Dinner:
- 1 cup apricot nectar (140)
- 1/2 broiled chicken breast (160)
- Hearty diet salad (63):
  - 1/4 head lettuce (18)
  - 1 tablespoon Italian diet dressing (8)
  - 1/2 cucumber (4) and medium tomato (33)
- 1/2 cup mashed potatoes (88)
- 1/2 cup plain, low-fat yogurt, with sprinkling of
  blueberries (85)
- Coffee or tea, no cream or sugar

Snack:
- 1/2 cup blueberries (45)
- 1/2 cup skim milk (44)

Remember: During the day, drink 8 8-ounce glasses of water.

Day 45

A merry heart does good, like medicine,/But a broken spirit dries the bones (Prov. 17:22).

Read Proverbs 17:19–24.

Much of what has been said in this book has focused on diet and exercise. Physicians and other scientists are beginning to understand that what goes on in the mind is just as important to good health as what goes on in the digestive tract, the blood, or the muscles. For many people, the presence of stress and the way they react to pressure may be the most important factors in their physical well-being.

Solomon understood this fact long before our contemporary stress experts were on the scene. He knew that a positive attitude—including a cheerful disposition and outlook on life—is essential to our good health. On the negative side, he understood that depression and anxiety, or what he called a "crushed spirit," would have a bad impact on our bodies.

I've found there are at least two ways to keep my spirits up and my heart cheerful, even in the face of the worst pressures of daily life. First of all, I *will* myself to thinking positively. I deliberately choose to concentrate on those things that are uplifting, and I push the negatives right out of my consciousness. Second, to reinforce my individual efforts, I try to spend a fair amount of time in the company of those who think positively, those who encourage me to stay buoyant and hopeful, no matter how gloomy things may seem.

I often remind myself of the old adage, "A positive confession works wonders! A negative confession makes matters worse!" My method doesn't always work, but its success rate proves to me the truth of Solomon's words.

Prayer: Lord, make me into a positive person. I want to be a realist, yet I also want to see the silver lining in every cloud that comes into my life.

Breakfast:
  1 cup skim milk (88)
  1/2 cup bran cereal (70)
  6 orange wedges (46)

Lunch:
  Fruit special:
    1/2 cup pineapple, avocado, and strawberries (100), over
    1/2 cup plain, low-fat yogurt (71)
  3 1/2 ounces roasted turkey, white meat (176)
  1/2 cup steamed cabbage (16)
  Coffee or tea, no cream or sugar

Dinner:
  1 cup strawberries (52)
  1 1/2 ounces broiled steak (128)
  Cucumber treat: 1 chopped cucumber (45), over one lettuce
    leaf and one large slice of tomato (10)
  1/4 cup mashed potatoes (44)
  1 cup skim milk (88)

Snack:
  1/2 cantaloupe (82)
  1/2 cup orange juice (56)

Remember: During the day, drink 8 8-ounce glasses of water.

Day 46

The spirit of a man will sustain him in sickness,/But who can bear a broken spirit? (Prov. 18:14).

Read Proverbs 18:1–14.

At one party I attended, I was shocked at the way one husband treated his wife. Every time she would try to contribute to the conversation, he would put her down in some way. I don't believe he realized what he was doing.

The impact on her was dramatic. She would stare at the table, not saying a word. A thought would come to her, and she would brighten up for a moment or two. Apparently gathering up her courage, she would say something which I always found to be quite interesting. The husband would always step in and criticize, and she would lapse back into silence; her gaze would return to the table. In these moments of rejection, her entire demeanor, the very features on her face, seemed to shrivel up.

In a later conversation with her, outside of her husband's hearing, I learned that she had been having some physical problems in recent years. In addition to high blood pressure, she developed colds during the winter months which she simply couldn't shake.

All I could think of was the verse in today's Bible meditation. This woman could hardly bear the burden of her husband's criticisms and disapproval. I strongly suspect that the ability of her body to fight off even the common cold had been lowered significantly.

Just observing the interaction between this husband and his wife impressed me with what an important responsibility each of us has for the attitudes, and also the physical health, of our friends and loved ones.

Prayer: Lord, help me become more aware of the positive or negative effect I have on the well-being of others. Show me how to uplift someone today by a kind word or touch.

Breakfast:
   1 cup orange juice (112)
   1 soft-boiled egg (80)
   1 slice whole wheat toast (61)
   1 cup skim milk (88)

Lunch:
   6-ounce glass tomato juice (35)
   2 ounces meat balls (156)
   1 cup summer squash (29)
   1 medium apple (86)

Dinner:
   1/2 roasted chicken breast (182)
   1 cup mixed vegetables (116)
   1/4 head of lettuce (18)
   1/2 tomato (16)
   1 cup skim milk (88)

Snack:
   1 papaya (119)
   2 walnuts (68)

Remember: During the day, drink 8 8-ounce glasses of water.

Day 47

Better is a dry morsel with quietness,/Than a house full
of feasting with strife (Prov. 17:1).

Read Proverbs 17:1–3.

One man was contrasting two of his recent meal experiences,
one quite positive and the other almost entirely negative. Ironi-
cally, the worst time was a Thanksgiving meal where a dozen or so
members of a family got together, supposedly to celebrate and
thank God for all their blessings. Unfortunately, most of the gathering involved bickering, arguments, and finally a serious rupture in
the relationship between two sisters.

The other meal was some sandwiches and soup he had shared
one night with his wife, alone in their kitchen. They talked on and
on as they munched on their meager fare, and both agreed it was
one of the most enjoyable "dates" they had ever experienced together.

Somehow those "feasts" which we prepare and to which we
attach our greatest expectations often seem to fall flat. But when
we focus on a relationship and cultivate it over a simple meal, a
kind of "divine surprise" may well break through into our lives.

Prayer: Dear God, enable me always to put human relationships in first place before any food that is served. Give me the grace
to anticipate problems that may develop in family gatherings and to
defuse explosive situations.

Breakfast:
   1 cup orange juice (112)
   1 slice whole wheat toast (61)
   1 soft-boiled egg (80)
   Coffee or tea, no cream or sugar

Lunch:
   3 ounces steamed shrimp (110)
   1 stalk steamed broccoli (47)
* ¼ cup cooked Brown and Wild Rice (44)

1-inch cube of melted cheddar cheese (over the broccoli) (68)
1 cup Indonesian pilaf (76)
Coffee or tea, no cream or sugar

Dinner:
   3 ounces lean ground beef (235)
   1/2 cup cooked cauliflower (60)
   1 cup tossed salad (20)
* 1 Surprise Roll (119)
   1 cup skim milk (88)

Snack:
   1/2 cup skim milk (44)

Remember: During the day, drink 8 8-ounce glasses of water.

Day 48

The person who labors, labors for himself,/For his hungry mouth drives him on (Prov. 16:26).

Read Proverbs 16:25–33.

A rather affluent young man shared with me that he led his family in saying grace before each meal. Even though he gave lip service to the words, "Thank You, God, for the food we are about to eat," he admitted that he didn't really *feel* thankful. He had sufficient income that he wasn't worried about not having enough to put food on his family's table.

Then he lost his job. For several weeks, his family relied on some savings they had accumulated. He remained optimistic that he would get another position soon. As a result, he still wasn't really worried about providing the basics of life, such as food, for his wife and children.

As months went by and his funds were depleted even further, he and his wife began to cut back on everything, including their daily menus. Sometimes they had to borrow to pay the rent and put food on the table. More often, as they prayed for help, money came in from unexpected sources: family gifts, surprise refunds on taxes, or part-time consulting assignments. Now, when he said grace and thanked God from day to day, he really meant it. He no longer knew exactly where the next meal was coming from.

Soon, he got another job, which paid just as much as his previous one. Never again did he question the significance of thanking God for each meal he ate. Always in the back of his mind were those hard times when God had literally been in charge of his family's daily diet.

Prayer: Lord, I thank You for giving me and my family the means to eat well each day. Show me how best to spend my food money so as to achieve maximum health. Help me to be truly thankful for all Your wonderful provisions for us.

Breakfast:
    1 cup orange juice (112)
    1 cup bran cereal (140)
    1 cup skim milk (88)
    $^{1}/_{2}$ cup black raspberries (49)
    Coffee or tea, no cream or sugar

Lunch:
    1 ounce natural cheese (107), melted over
    1 slice whole wheat bread (61)
    12 fresh lettuce leaves (9)
    $^{1}/_{2}$ fresh tomato (16)
    1 tablespoon diet salad dressing (35)
    Coffee or tea, no cream or sugar

Dinner:
* 1 cup Chili with Beans (180)
* $^{1}/_{4}$ cup cooked Brown and Wild Rice (44)
    $^{1}/_{2}$ cup plain, low-fat yogurt, with sprinkling of strawberry slices (85)
* $^{1}/_{2}$ cup Grapefruit-Avocado Salad (98)
    Coffee or tea, no cream or sugar

Snack:
    1 cup fresh, unsweetened fruit cocktail (91)
    1 cup skim milk (88)

Remember: During the day, drink 8 8-ounce glasses of water.

Day 49

Pleasant words are like a honeycomb,/Sweetness to the soul and health to the bones (Prov. 16:24).

Read Proverbs 16:20–25.

Undisciplined snacking is the bane of the dieter's existence. I always try to look for the most attractive, compelling substitutes I can find to put in the place of food at those times when I'm most inclined to snack.

One approach is to reach for the Bible and turn to a favorite passage of Scripture. Another way is to pull out my exercise togs and go for a vigorous walk, run, or swim.

Perhaps the most effective antidote to the snack syndrome, especially when other people are participating as part of a coffee break or home get-together, is to focus on the conversation instead of the food. In other words, for your next coffee break, resolve to take *only* coffee or tea and then substitute the words of others for the sweets.

If you get into the habit of taking your coffee breaks this way, I think you'll find yourself invigorated by more stimulating conversation and enhanced personal relationships. You'll also find yourself taking in fewer unnecessary calories.

Prayer: Dear God, I thank You for all the friends You've given me. Help me to pay more attention to them, and whenever possible, help me to concentrate on them instead of my food.

Breakfast:
  1/2 cup orange juice (56)
  1 cornmeal pancake (68)
  1 teaspoon margarine (35)
  1 tablespoon honey (61)
  1 cup skim milk (88)
  Coffee or tea, no cream or sugar

Lunch:
   1/2 cup lentil soup (150)
   1 ounce natural cheese cubes (107), over
   1/2 slice rye bread (40)
   1 cup skim milk (88)

Dinner:
   1 medium apple with skin (86)
   1 cup fish chowder (100)
   1/2 ounce cheese (55)
   3 wheat crackers (50)
   1/4 head of lettuce (18)
   1 teaspoon Italian diet dressing (8)
   1/2 cup skim milk (44)
   Coffee or tea, no cream or sugar

Snack:
   1/4 cup fresh blueberries (22), over
   1/2 cup plain, low-fat yogurt (71)

Remember: During the day, drink 8 8-ounce glasses of water.

Day 50

Better is a dinner of herbs where love is,/Than a fatted calf with hatred (Prov. 15:17).

Read Proverbs 15:13–20.

There are two points that strike home with me in this verse. First of all, I think it's essential to try to resolve all disputes within your family before you sit down to eat. There's nothing more destructive to the digestion, and I believe to the health, than to eat a meal where each mouthful ends as a knot in your stomach because of the tension at the table. If you can't resolve a dispute, it may at least be helpful to declare a temporary "truce" until after the meal has been finished.

Second, even if you don't have a problem with tension or hatred at your meals, it's still advisable to emphasize "herbs"—or "vegetables," as the word is sometimes translated in the above verse—in your daily diet. Why? Animal meat contains fats that are associated with coronary heart disease.

Clearly, a verse like this is packed with meaning, both nutritional and spiritual. So I try never to read the Proverbs quickly. It always pays great dividends for my practical well-being to linger over Solomon's words.

Prayer: Father, help me to provide a calming, stabilizing influence at our family meals. Give us a special blessing of peace at our table.

Breakfast:
   1/2 cup cantaloupe balls and strawberries (55)
   1 oatmeal muffin (96)
   1 teaspoon margarine (35)
   1 cup skim milk (88)

Lunch:
   1/2 cup orange sections (62)
   1 serving salmon loaf (198)
   1 cup tossed vegetable salad (60), with

1 teaspoon olive oil dressing (35)
1/2 cup skim milk (44)
1 cup honeydew melon (52)

Dinner:
3 ounces steamed shrimp (110)
* 1/4 cup cooked Brown and Wild Rice (44)
4 slices tomato (10)
1 nectarine (37)

Snack:
1/2 cup plain, low-fat yogurt (71)
1/3 medium banana (34)

Remember: During the day, drink 8 8-ounce glasses of water.

Day 51

A sound heart is life to the body,/But envy is rottenness
to the bones (Prov. 14:30).

Read Proverbs 14:29–35.

The heart, in biblical terms, is the center of our distinctive human nature—our will, our emotions, our very identity. A heart that is sound, one that is at peace and is oriented toward God, will have a positive effect on the rest of the body, including the physical organ we call the heart.

On the other hand, any negative emotions, especially those that tend to gnaw away at us day in and day out, will disturb our peace. They may also jeopardize the well-being of our physical hearts. In my experience, envy is one of the most destructive of those negative feelings.

I'm reminded of a man, John, who became extremely jealous because a college classmate, who had entered the same field, was doing much better than he was. The classmate was earning more money and had gotten more promotions than John—so many, in fact, that it seemed John could never catch up to him.

John thought about his classmate almost every day of his life, and envy is the only word for the dominant emotion that gripped him. As a result, he frequently looked drawn and tense, and he became more and more snappish around his family.

Finally, John's wife told him, "This is ridiculous! This man is ruining your life and ours as well. You're shriveling up inside because of him, and you haven't even been in touch with him for several years. It's ironic because he has no idea what he's doing to you. Why don't you try calling him? I'll bet you'd find you really have nothing to be so envious about."

Finally, John did as his wife suggested. He found that his classmate was indeed quite successful but was also as miserable as John himself, but for a different reason. Although the other man had nearly reached the top of his field, he found it was more boring and less satisfying than he had thought. This meeting freed John from his bondage to envy and showed him he really needed to look for meaning in life apart from his drive to succeed on the job.

Prayer: Lord, help me to root out the most destructive emotions and feelings in my life. Show me what steps I can take to find more peace.

Breakfast:
   1/2 cup apple cider (58)
   1 scrambled egg (82)
   1 slice whole wheat bread (61)
   Coffee or tea, no cream or sugar

Lunch:
   1/2 cup bean soup (60)
   3 ounces roast pork (274)
   1 cup zucchini (33)
   1 plum (22)
   Coffee or tea, no cream or sugar

Dinner:
   1/2 cup grapefruit and mandarin orange sections (40)
   1 slice avocado pear (80), sprinkled with
   2 tablespoons coconut and nuts (90)
   1 cup skim milk (88)
   3 ounces broiled or roasted veal (200)
*   1/4 cup cooked Brown and Wild Rice (44)
   Coffee or tea, no cream or sugar

Snack:
   2 fresh peaches (76)

Remember: During the day, drink 8 8-ounce glasses of water.

Day 52

Hope deferred makes the heart sick,/But when the desire comes, it is a tree of life (Prov. 13:12).

Read Proverbs 13:9–14.

One of the most stressful circumstances I know is the situation where we want something desperately, but for some reason we can't get it.

Obviously, if it's possible to satisfy a legitimate desire or hope, the best advice is to take concrete steps to achieve it. The anxiety you may feel, say, about having a clean house or reviving a lapsed friendship, may be mostly "reactive," as the psychologists would say. That is, your inner discomfort may stem mainly from your failure to act in ways that are within your power.

Sometimes you have no control over the fulfillment of your hopes. You may want to get married, but the right mate just doesn't come along. Or you may want a particular job in a very restricted field, such as acting or the arts, and no openings appear.

The only healthy approach to these difficult situations is to pray that God will teach you how to wait. Ask Him to show you what productive thoughts and activities you can pursue in the interim. In fact, ask Him to make this waiting period even more meaningful and satisfying than the hoped-for object that you feel has been deferred. Also, ask that God will draw closer to you during this time and show you more about Himself than you've ever known before.

In this way, stress will decrease and may even disappear entirely. You'll have learned something about your own spiritual life, and you'll be in a much better position to deal with similar deferrals of hope in the future.

Prayer: Lord, I thank You for the times You require me to wait for answers to prayer because I know You have something important to teach me before I receive Your full blessings.

Breakfast:
  6-ounce glass tomato juice (35)
  1 cup bran cereal (140)
  1 cup skim milk (88)
  4 cherries (13)
  Coffee or tea, no cream or sugar

Lunch:
  3 ounces pot roast (222)
  1 cup steamed cabbage (36)
  1 teaspoon margarine (35)
  1 cup skim milk (88)
  1/2 cup watermelon (32)

Dinner:
  1 cup apple cider (60)
  4 ounces baked flounder (230)
  1 cup steamed broccoli (58)
  1 teaspoon margarine (35)
  1/2 banana (50)

Snack:
  1/2 cup plain, low-fat yogurt (71), topped with
  1 fresh peach (38)

Remember: During the day, drink 8 8-ounce glasses of water.

Day 53

A generous soul will be made rich,/And he who waters
will also be watered himself (Prov. 11:25).

Read Proverbs 11:24–26.

When we give something of our worldly goods to others, we
almost always seem to get more in return, though our rewards may
not be quite what we have expected.

Take the sharing of food, for example. A New York businessman invited a "street person," a poor man who lived on the urban
streets, to dine at his apartment. Some of the businessman's friends
said, "Oh, you'd better be careful—he may steal you blind," or,
"You never know what diseases he may be carrying."

The businessman was unfazed. One meal led to another and
another until the two, despite their divergent backgrounds, became rather good friends. The poor man, of course, benefitted because he got some free meals, occasional used clothing, and other
material gifts.

But there was much more involved than just the passing of
presents. The businessman, a Christian, was able to share his faith
with the poor man, and as a result, the street person left the streets,
took up gainful employment, and actually made a commitment of
his life to Jesus Christ.

The businessman may have received even more from the relationship than he gave. His eyes were opened to the plight of those
who were much less fortunate than he himself, and he became
more responsive to others in need.

These spiritual rewards for both men came as a direct result of
one simple meal, shared with no thought of what might be gained
in return.

Prayer: Lord, lead me to someone today who needs material
help. Help me to understand how I can share creatively the blessings You have given me.

Breakfast:
>   1 slice rye bread (61)
>   1 soft-boiled egg (80)
>   1 wedge honeydew melon (49)
>   1 cup orange juice (112)
>   1/2 cup skim milk (44)

Lunch:
>   3 ounces steamed shrimp (110)
>   1 cup steamed cauliflower (27)
>   1 slice whole wheat bread (61)
>   1/2 cup skim milk (44)

Dinner:
>   1/2 chicken breast, broiled, baked, or boiled (160)
>   1 cup mushrooms (20)
>   1 cup snap beans (60)
>   1/2 cup cooked brown rice (70)
>   1 cup skim milk (88)
>   1 fresh ear boiled corn on the cob (70)

Snack:
>   1/2 cup watermelon (32)

Remember: During the day, drink 8 8-ounce glasses of water.

Day 54

The fear of the LORD prolongs days,/But the years of the wicked will be shortened (Prov. 10:27).

Read Proverbs 10:27–32.

There are many promises of long life in the Bible, and I've often wondered if perhaps there is some health-oriented reason for these assurances of longevity.

The more I've thought about it, the more I've become convinced that a life with God, a life that puts Him in first place, is a life that tends to be more balanced, meaningful, and filled with inner peace. Specifically, a life with God, which rests on solid faith and trust in Him, does at least three important things for our health.

First, faith gives us a more positive outlook on situations. Mature Christians tend to look on the bright side of life, and they expect God to help them work through various problems they may be facing. Second, with Jesus as our constant friend, there is a ready spiritual source to overcome feelings of depression or anxiety. We are told in the Scriptures that we should cast our cares on Him because He cares for us. These two very practical "safety valves" for pressure and worry must enhance health.

Third, faith gives us something to hope for, something to look forward to, in this life and in the life to come. Those who have studied patients with cancer and other terminal illnesses have discovered that people with a positive, hopeful attitude—and the will to live—usually live longer than those with a more defeatist outlook.

Having a "fear of the Lord" isn't only something that is good for longevity; there are eternal dimensions to faith that go far beyond our physical well-being. There's no doubt in my mind that faith has important implications for our health in this life as well. Our relationship with God is something that begins to work in our favor now and continues into the infinite recesses of eternity.

Prayer: Dear God, show me how to take care of my body so that I can live the maximum number of years You have allotted to me. I thank You for providing the inner peace, freedom from anxiety, and meaning in life that would be impossible without Your presence.

Breakfast:
   1 grapefruit (110)
   1 slice whole wheat toast (61)
   ¹/₂ cup bran cereal (70)
   1 cup orange juice (112)

Lunch:
   2 stalks celery (14)
   3 ounces ground beef (235)
   1 slice whole wheat bread (61)
   ¹/₂ cup skim milk (44)

Dinner:
   3 ounces roasted lamb (231)
* ¹/₄ cup cooked Brown and Wild Rice (44)
* 1 cup Cucumber-Mint Salad (46)
   ¹/₂ cup skim milk (44)
   1 cup asparagus (52)

Snack:
   ¹/₄ cup fresh melon (13)

Remember: During the day, drink 8 8-ounce glasses of water.

Day 55

As cold water to a weary soul,/So is good news from a far country (Prov. 25:25).

Read Proverbs 25:21–28.

Fresh, cool water has always served as a cornerstone of good health. All of us have been very thirsty many times in our lives, and we know quite well the truth of the image that King Solomon portrays in the above saying.

One of the most important elements in a good diet is water. If a person goes without sufficient liquids for very long, he begins to get irritable and sluggish and may even suffer more serious health problems from dehydration. In fact, if a person goes without any liquids at all for about three days, he will die. For this reason, anyone who has embarked on a fast should always be warned to drink plenty of water or juice.

In my New You diet, I recommend that you drink eight eight-ounce glasses of water each day. In this way, you'll be sure to get plenty of liquids into your system, and you'll also leave less room in your stomach for high-calorie foods.

Prayer: Lord, I thank You for providing me with plenty of fresh, healthful water. Teach me more about the "living water" that Your Son Jesus also has offered to me.

Breakfast:
　　1 cup melon (52)
　　1 slice oatmeal bread (60)
　　1 teaspoon margarine (35)
　　1 cup skim milk (88)
　　Coffee or tea, no cream or sugar

Lunch:
　　3 ounces cooked crab meat (90)
　　1 cup fruit salad (120)
　　1 ounce natural cheese (107), melted over
　　1 slice whole wheat bread (61)
　　Coffee or tea, no cream or sugar

Dinner:

   2 ounces broiled sirloin steak (175)
   1/4 cup cooked mushrooms and tomatoes (28)
   1 baked potato (76)
   1 cup spinach salad (30)
   1 teaspoon diet Italian dressing (8)

Snack:

   1 fresh nectarine (36)
   1/2 cup plain, low-fat yogurt (71)

Remember: During the day, drink 8 8-ounce glasses of water.

Day 56

Honor the Lord with your possessions,/And with the firstfruits of all your increase;/So your barns will be filled with plenty,/And your vats will overflow with new wine (Prov. 3:9–10).

Read Proverbs 3:1–10.

In Old Testament times, when agriculture was the main industry, people who followed and obeyed God would typically contribute the best of their produce to Him.

Today, those who are His people more often give money to His service, but there are still important steps we can take to dedicate our food.

If your church or community has a food program for the poor, you might buy some extra canned goods to contribute each time you go out shopping. By the biblical standard, these foods you give away should be as good, healthful, and tasty as anything you buy and eat yourself.

As you sit down at the dinner table, you might pray that the food you are about to eat will build you up physically. Ask God to give you added energy, so that you will be better prepared to serve Him. In this way, you will in a sense be giving Him the "firstfruits," as you focus on improving the well-being of His temple, which is your body.

Prayer: Lord, show me new and more meaningful ways that I can serve You and give to Your work. Even as I understand what You want me to do with my life, give me the physical energy and spiritual power to achieve Your objectives.

Breakfast:
  1 cup orange juice (112)
  1 cup wheat and oat cereal (159)
  1 cup skim milk (88)

Lunch:
    Special turkey sandwich (258):
        3 ounces turkey, light meat (150), on
        1 slice whole wheat bread (61), covered with
        1 stalk cooked broccoli (47)
    1 small pear (56)
    Coffee or tea, no cream or sugar

Dinner:
    1 cup watermelon (42)
    3 ounces 100 percent lean, boneless beef flank (167)
    1 cup tomatoes, cucumbers, and lettuce (20)
    1 medium boiled ear of corn (70)
    Coffee or tea, no cream or sugar

Snack:
    1 cup fresh strawberries (52)
    1/2 cup melon (26)

Remember: During the day, drink 8 8-ounce glasses of water.

The Home Stretch!

Now, you are about to begin the last two weeks of your New You diet program. Your objective has been to break down the barriers that separate your physical and spiritual being so that a healthy, low-calorie diet becomes an integral part of your basic philosophy of life. Only in this way, as you begin to see that God Himself wants to get you in good physical shape, can you hope to make permanent those weight losses and improvements in your fitness.

To this end of achieving long-term good health and proper weight, I've found it's essential to have certain spiritual principles at my fingertips. If I can call to mind exactly what God has said about food, exercise, and good health in general, I'm in a much better position to pray effectively and take advantage of the promises and guidelines He has provided.

The best way for me to make God's principles a part of my very being is first to memorize relevant passages in His book, the Bible. Then if I periodically meditate on these verses, I find they are readily accessible when questions or temptations arise in my mind about food, exercise, or other health concerns.

For the last two weeks of the New You diet, I have chosen to focus on fourteen key verses, which I would like you to memorize and meditate upon each day. Spend at least ten minutes on each short verse and meditation. Work first at memorizing the verse; then hold the verse and the thought that follows it in your mind. Mull them over; allow God's Spirit to show you any special meanings they may have for you personally. In this way, you'll be "armed" with the greatest spiritual weapon available—God's written Word. As you move away from this book back into the challenges of daily living and eating, you'll be much more likely to maintain the healthier weight and physical condition you have finally reached.

Day 57

Memory verse: "Man shall not live by bread alone, but by every word that proceeds from the mouth of God" (Matt. 4:4).

Meditation: Bible reading is a way of escape from the temptations of food.

Breakfast:
    ¹/₂ grapefruit (55)
* 1 Love Waffle (90)
    1 teaspoon honey (61)
    1 cup skim milk (88)

Lunch:
    3 ounces boneless roasted beef (278)
    1 cup steamed green beans (30)
    Sunshine salad (191):
        1 cup fresh strawberries (52)
        ¹/₄ cup avocado and pineapples (64), on
        1 lettuce leaf (4), topped with
        ¹/₂ cup plain, low-fat yogurt (71)

Dinner:
    4 ounces sliced turkey breast (208)
    1 cup steamed broccoli (58)
    ¹/₂ cup cooked cauliflower (24)
* ¹/₃ cup cooked Brown and Wild Rice (58)

Snack:
    ¹/₂ cup skim milk (44)

Remember: During the day, drink 8 8-ounce glasses of water.

Day 58

Memory verse: "Whoever drinks of the water that I shall give him will never thirst" (John 4:14).

Meditation: Drink fresh water each day for the body and "living water" each day for the spirit.

Breakfast:
　　1 cup orange juice (112)
　　1 cup bran cereal (140)
　　1 cup skim milk (88)
　　1 cup fresh strawberries (52)

Lunch:
　　Chef's salad and vinegar (177):
　　　　1 head lettuce (36)
　　　　12 slices cucumber (8)
　　　　1 tomato (33)
　　　　3 slices cold cuts (100)
　　1 pumpernickel bagel (140)

Dinner:
　　1/2 roasted chicken breast (182)
　　1 cup cooked carrots (40)
　　1 cup skim milk (88)
　　1 baked potato, 1-2 1/2 inches in diameter (76)

Snack:
　　1 fresh sliced peach (38)
　　1/2 cup plain, low-fat yogurt (71)

Remember: During the day, drink 8 8-ounce glasses of water.

Day 59

Memory verse: "I am the bread of life. He who comes to Me shall never hunger, and he who believes in Me shall never thirst" (John 6:35).

Meditation: Ask Jesus for help when you face problems sticking to your diet.

Breakfast:
  1 cup orange juice (112)
  ¹/₂ cup hot oatmeal (74)
  1 cup skim milk (88)

Lunch:
  Tuna salad plate (170):
    3¹/₂ ounces tuna, canned in water (127)
    1 medium tomato cut in squares (33)
    1 teaspoon green pepper mixed with onions and
      celery, finely chopped (10)
  Coffee or tea, no cream or sugar

Dinner:
  3 ounces broiled steak (260)
* ¹/₄ cup cooked Brown and Wild Rice (44)
  1 baked potato, 1-2¹/₂ inches in diameter (76)
  12 spears asparagus (36)
  ³/₄ cup fruit salad: strawberries, avocado,
    and pineapple (63)
  ¹/₂ cup plain, low-fat yogurt (71)
  Coffee or tea, no cream or sugar

Snack:
  1 cup fresh strawberries (52)
  ¹/₂ cup apple juice (58)

Remember: During the day, drink 8 8-ounce glasses of water.

Day 60

Memory verse: "Give us this day our daily bread" (Matt. 6:11).

Meditation: Eat only what is necessary for your best health.

Breakfast:
1 cup grapefruit juice (96)
1 poached egg (80)
1 slice whole wheat toast (61)
Coffee or tea, no cream or sugar

Lunch:
4 ounces broiled or poached halibut filet (214)
2 stalks broccoli (94)
1 cube cheddar cheese (68)
Decaffeinated diet soft drink

Dinner:
1 cup snap beans (60)
3 ounces broiled sirloin steak (260)
1/2 cup skim milk (44)
1 medium apple (86)
1 baked potato, 1-2 1/2 inches in diameter (76)
Coffee or tea, no cream or sugar

Snack:
1/2 cup skim milk (44)
6 grapes (25)

Remember: During the day, drink 8 8-ounce glasses of water.

Day 61

Memory verse: "Therefore I say to you, do not worry about your life, what you will eat or what you will drink; nor about your body, what you will put on. Is not life more than food and the body more than clothing?" (Matt. 6:25).

Meditation: There are so many things in my life that are more important than food. They include: (List those things which are more important, and thank God for them).

Breakfast:
   $^1/_2$ cup apricot juice (61)
   1 banana bran muffin (120)
   1 soft-boiled egg (80)
   1 cup skim milk (88)
   Coffee or tea, no cream or sugar

Lunch:
   3 ounces mixed broiled seafood (170): halibut,
      codfish, haddock
* $^1/_2$ cup cooked Brown and Wild Rice (44)
   1 cup tossed salad (20)
   $^1/_2$ cup grapefruit and mandarin orange sections (81)
   Coffee or tea, no cream or sugar

Dinner:
   3 ounces baked fish in cheese (228)
   1 cup cooked yellow squash (52)
   1 cup skim milk (88)

Snack:
   1 medium apple (86)

Remember: During the day, drink 8 8-ounce glasses of water.

Day 62

Memory verse: "For I was hungry and you gave Me food; I was thirsty and you gave Me drink; I was a stranger and you took Me in" (Matt. 25:35).

Meditation: When we give food to a needy person, we give it to Christ. When tempted to buy food we shouldn't eat, why not put that money into a fund for the needy?

Breakfast:
　　1 wedge honeydew melon (49)
　　1 cup Bird Seed Cereal (110)
　　1 cup skim milk (88)
　　Coffee or tea, no cream or sugar

Lunch:
　　3 ounces broiled veal chuck (200)
　　1 cup zucchini (33)
　　1 piece watermelon (111)
*　　1/2 cup Green Salad (10)
　　Coffee or tea, no cream or sugar

Dinner:
　　1/2 baked or broiled chicken breast (160)
　　1 cup mixed vegetables (116)
　　1 baked potato, 1-2 1/2 inches in diameter (76)
　　1 slice whole wheat bread (61)
　　1 cup cooked green beans (60)
　　1 sliced peach (38), over
　　1/4 cup plain, low-fat yogurt (35)

Snack:
　　1 cup skim milk (88)

Remember: During the day, drink 8 8-ounce glasses of water.

Day 63

Memory verse: "Do you not know that your body is the temple of the Holy Spirit who is in you, whom you have from God, and you are not your own?" (1 Cor. 6:19).

Meditation: God actually lives inside my body.

Breakfast:
 1 cup orange juice (112)
 1 soft-boiled egg (80)
 1 slice whole wheat toast (61)
 Coffee or tea, no cream or sugar

Lunch:
 1 cup vegetable soup (138)
 3 ounces ground beef (235)
 1 tomato (33)
 1/4 cup boiled wild rice (60)
 1/2 cup skim milk (44)

Dinner:
 3 1/2 ounces broiled swordfish steak (174)
 1 cup cooked, diced carrots (40)
 1 cup tossed lettuce and tomato salad (20)
 1 cup skim milk (88)

Snack:
 1 small bunch of seedless grapes (51)

Remember: During the day, drink 8 8-ounce glasses of water.

Day 64

Memory verse: "It is vain for you to rise up early,/ To sit up late,/To eat the bread of sorrows;/For so He gives His beloved sleep" (Ps. 127:2).

Meditation: God will resolve my problems if I give them to the Lord—and don't take them back. With this confidence I can now sleep.

Breakfast:
   6 orange wedges (46)
   1 cup bran cereal (140)
   1 cup skim milk (88)

Lunch:
   3 ounces broiled veal (200)
   1 cup mixed vegetables (116)
   6-ounce glass tomato juice (35)
   Coffee or tea, no cream or sugar

Dinner:
   1/2 cup fresh strawberries (26)
   1 ounce natural cheese (107)
   1 cup steamed broccoli (58)
   1 baked potato, 1-2 1/2 inches in diameter (76)
   1 cup skim milk (88)
   3 ounces broiled sirloin steak (260)
 * 1 serving Red, White, and Blue Dessert (40)
   Coffee or tea, no cream or sugar

Snack:
   1/2 cup plain, low-fat yogurt (71)

Remember: During the day, drink 8 8-ounce glasses of water.

Day 65

Memory verse: "For bodily exercise profits a little, but godliness is profitable for all things, having promise of the life that now is and of that which is to come" (1 Tim. 4:8).

Meditation: God is in charge of my exercise, my food, and my whole being. Lord, please help me to be more like Jesus in all that I do.

Breakfast:
  ¹/₂ cup orange juice (56)
  1 slice lean, crisp bacon (86)
  1 poached egg (80)
  1 slice whole wheat toast (61)

Lunch:
  ¹/₂ broiled tarragon chicken breast (160) (Sprinkle
    tarragon lightly over chicken before broiling.)
  ¹/₂ sliced cucumber (20)
  3 leaves lettuce (20)
  1 tomato, raw (33)
  1 cup skim milk (88)

Dinner:
  5 ounces boiled shrimp (183)
  1 cup broccoli (94)
* ¹/₂ cup cooked Brown and Wild Rice (44)
  ¹/₂ cup spinach (39)
  1 cup skim milk (88)

Snack:
  ¹/₂ cup fresh blueberries (45)

Remember: During the day, drink 8 8-ounce glasses of water.

Day 66

Memory verse: "Commit your works to the LORD,/And your thoughts will be established" (Prov. 16:3).

Meditation: Commit all your meals and exercise activities to God the first thing each morning during your devotions.

Breakfast:
   ¹/₂ cup bran cereal (70)
   1 cup skim milk (88)
   1 peach (38)

Lunch:
   6-ounce glass tomato juice (35)
   3-ounce hamburger patty (235)
   1 diced cucumber (41)
   1 tablespoon Italian diet dressing (8)
   ¹/₂ cup plain, low-fat yogurt (71), over
      10 seedless grapes (18)

Dinner:
   1 6-ounce halibut filet (169)
   1 cup steamed broccoli (58)
   1 cube cheddar cheese (68)
   1 boiled potato with parsley (80)

Snack:
   ¹/₂ cantaloupe (82)

Remember: During the day, drink 8 8-ounce glasses of water.

Day 67

Memory verse: "Be anxious for nothing, but in everything by prayer and supplication, with thanksgiving, let your requests be made known to God; and the peace of God, which surpasses all understanding, will guard your hearts and minds through Christ Jesus" (Phil 4:6–7).

Meditation: Prayer is the way to the peace of Christ, and inner peace is the best antidote to the frustrations that cause me to break my diet. Dear Lord, help me with my diet and exercise. Guard my mouth as well as my heart and mind.

Breakfast:
    10 cherries (58)
    1 soft-boiled egg (80)
    1/2 whole wheat English muffin (65)
    1 cup skim milk (88)

Lunch:
    Tuna salad plate (165):
        1 tomato (33), sliced over
        1 1/4 ounces tuna (64),
        1 teaspoon mayonnaise (50),
        1 tablespoon diced green pepper, onion, and
            celery (18)
    1 cup plain, low-fat yogurt, mixed in blender with
        1/4 cup strawberries, pear, and banana (146)

Dinner:
    1/2 cup cranberry juice (82)
    3 ounces sirloin steak (260)
    1/2 cup sliced carrots (22)
    1 leaf lettuce (10)
    1 tomato (33)
*   1/4 cup cooked Brown and Wild Rice (44)
    1/2 cup strawberries and melon dices (26)

Snack:
$^1/_2$ cup plain, low-fat yogurt (71)
1 tablespoon raisins (29)

Remember: During the day, drink 8 8-ounce glasses of water.

Day 68

Memory verse: "And God said, 'See, I have given you every herb that yields seed which is on the face of all the earth, and every tree whose fruit yields seed; to you it shall be for food' " (Gen. 1:29).

Meditation: God has given vegetables and fruits a special place in my diet. He will help me take advantage of them to satisfy my desire for food.

Breakfast:
    1 cup melon and red raspberries (67)
    1 soft-boiled egg (80)
    1 small corn muffin (56)

Lunch:
*   1 cup Carrot and Orange Soup (90)
    4 ounces low-fat cottage cheese (112)
    1 cup mixed fruit salad (94)
*   1 slice Surprise Bread (119)

Dinner:
    3 ounces loin veal (200)
*   1 cup Ratatouille (50)
    1 baked potato, 1-2½ inches in diameter (76)
    2 1-inch cubes of cheddar cheese (136)
    1 boiled ear of corn (70)
*   1 cup Green Salad (20)

Snack:
    1 fresh peach (38)

Remember: During the day, drink 8 8-ounce glasses of water.

Day 69

Memory verse: "I can do all things through Christ who strengthens me" (Phil. 4:13).

Meditation: Christ is the source of my power to maintain a healthy weight and keep up my exercise.

Breakfast:
   1 blueberry muffin (112)
   1 cup skim milk (88)
   1 cup grapefruit juice (96)
   Coffee or tea, no cream or sugar

Lunch:
   3¹/₂ ounces broiled swordfish steak (174)
   1 cup mixed vegetables (116)
* ¹/₄ cup cooked Brown and Wild Rice (44)
   Coffee or tea, no cream or sugar

Dinner:
   3¹/₂ ounces sliced turkey breast (176)
   ¹/₂ cup snap beans (30)
   1 cup cooked carrots (40)
   1 cup skim milk (88)

Snack:
   1 cup black raspberries (98)
   ¹/₂ cup plain, low-fat yogurt (71)

Remember: During the day, drink 8 8-ounce glasses of water.

Day 70

Memory verse: "I have not departed from the commandment of His lips; I have treasured the words of His mouth more than my necessary food" (Job 23:12).

Meditation: God's words must guide my New You diet and exercise program. They must help me to continue to keep my body a fit temple for the Holy Spirit.

Breakfast:
  1 cup bran cereal (140)
  6-ounce glass cranapple juice (129)
  1 cup skim milk (88)
  Coffee or tea, no cream or sugar

Lunch:
  3 ounces canned salmon (120)
  1 cube cheddar cheese (68), melted over
  1 slice whole wheat bread (61)
  8 leaves of lettuce (6)
  Coffee or tea, no cream or sugar

Dinner:
  3 ounces broiled veal (200)
  1/2 cup mixed vegetables (58)
  1/3 cup brown rice (58)
* 1 serving Spanish Cream (76)
  1/2 cup fresh strawberries (26)

Snack No. 1:
  1/4 cantaloupe (41)

Snack No. 2:
  1 fresh peach (38)

Remember: During the day, drink 8 8-ounce glasses of water.

CHAPTER FIVE

A Guide to Dede's Elegant Diet Dishes

T hroughout this book you've been introduced to a variety of healthful, low-calorie foods. Some of the dishes mentioned have been marked with asterisks (*), and I've included descriptions of how to prepare those foods in this recipe section. It's easy to prepare these delicious diet meals; as a matter of fact, I regularly make them for Pat, our family, and friends.

As we will see in the latter part of this section, many of the recipes can also be adapted for elegant, low-calorie entertaining. Indeed, the proper combination of these foods can provide just the right counterpoint for the most special culinary occasions in your home.

But first, here are the recipes for the foods we have included throughout our New You diet plan.

BIRD SEED CEREAL

Pat and I have found several low-calorie cold cereals and grains to be delicious when served with skim milk or yogurt and frozen, sugarless berries. Blueberries and raspberries are our special favorites.

This particular concoction is one of our favorite morning cereals. We laughingly call it bird seed, but if this is eating like a bird, I'm all for it.

1 cup sesame seed
1 cup pumpkin seed

1 cup sunflower seed
2 cups 7-grain cereal or rolled oats
1 cup sliced almonds
2 cups bran
1 cup lecithin
1 cup wheat germ
2 cups raisins
1 cup coconut
2 teaspoons cinnamon

Mix all ingredients together and spread out onto two cookie sheets. Dribble 1 tablespoon of sunflower oil over the mixture on each sheet and bake at 275° for thirty minutes, stirring occasionally. Store mixture in an airtight jar or container. When serving, simply add a small amount to one tablespoon of low-fat, plain yogurt. As a topping, use finely chopped apple or berries, and sprinkle with brewer's yeast to taste. (One 1-cup serving = 110 calories)

TOMATO ICE

4 cups tomato juice
12 ounces Perrier
1 cup lemon juice
4 egg whites
Freshly ground black pepper, to taste
Fresh dill (garnish)

Process all the ingredients in a blender, or a food processor fitted with a steel blade. Taste and correct the seasonings. Pour into ice cube trays or other freezer containers, and freeze overnight. If time allows, freeze the mixture completely. Then, remove and process the mixture once more in the blender or food processor to break up the ice crystals, and refreeze. The mixture will now be slightly slushy, so you can easily spoon it into individual serving glasses and garnish on top with fresh dill. Makes eight servings. (One 6-ounce serving = 32 calories)

MINTED FRESH FRUIT

1 pint strawberries
3 kiwi fruits
1 medium ripe cantaloupe

1 medium ripe honeydew melon
Handful of fresh mint leaves
$1/2$ cup orange juice
$1/4$ cup lemon juice
3 packets artificial sweetener

Wash and hull the strawberries. Make melon balls from both melons, and peel and slice the kiwis, reserving one sliced kiwi to use as a garnish. Mix all the fruits together. Finely chop three-quarters of the mint leaves and stems, and sprinkle over the fruit. Reserve the remaining mint leaves to use as a garnish.

Mix the orange juice and the lemon juice together and pour over the fruit mixture. Toss gently but thoroughly.

Arrange the remaining kiwi slices on top, garnish with the remaining mint sprigs, and chill for two to three hours. Serve cold. Makes twelve servings. (One l-cup serving = 84 calories)

FRUIT DIP (OR FRUIT SALAD DRESSING)

1 cup plain, low-fat yogurt
2 tablespoons concentrated frozen orange juice
1 tablespoon honey

Simply mix the ingredients together, and refrigerate until ready to serve with a platter of fresh fruit. (One $1/4$–cup serving = 40 calories)

OMELET

This versatile dish can be made with a variety of delicious low-calorie toppings or fillings to suit any occasion. To keep calories to a minimum, make the omelet in the usual manner, but use a vegetable-based nonstick spray in the pan instead of butter.

Omelet toppings and fillings can be prepared ahead for a group and kept warm in a chafing dish over hot water. Omelets can be made individually with each topping; but when serving a group, it is sometimes easier to make a number of plain omelets with a lengthwise slit so that everyone can custom-make his own. Here are some of our favorite crowd-pleasing toppings:

1. *Cinnamon apples*—Sauté apples in nonstick vegetable spray with cinnamon, and add a dash of nutmeg before serving.

2. *Sautéed mushrooms*—Sauté mushrooms in nonstick veg-

etable spray. As they begin to wilt, add a few splashes of sherry or red cooking wine.

3. *Watercress*—Sauté watercress briefly in nonstick vegetable spray, just until wilted. Roll into omelet.

4. *Cheddar cheese*—Sprinkle grated cheese onto omelet as it cooks.

5. *Ratatouille*—Prepare ratatouille (recipe below), and spoon onto omelet mixture as it cooks.

(One omelet with assorted toppings = 92 calories)

RATATOUILLE

This vegetable treat is too good to use only for omelets. It is a healthful and hearty side dish that is a welcome addition to any meal.

1 cup olive oil
4 small eggplants, cut into 1½ inch cubes
1½ pounds onions, peeled and chopped
7 medium zucchini, cut into 2-inch strips
2 medium sweet red peppers, seeded, cut into ½-inch strips
2 medium bell peppers, seeded, cut into ½-inch strips
2 tablespoons minced garlic
3 16-ounce cans Italian plum tomatoes, drained
1 can tomato paste
¼ cup Italian parsley, chopped
¼ cup chopped fresh dill
2 tablespoons dried basil
2 tablespoons dried oregano
Freshly ground pepper

Preheat oven to 400°. Line a large roasting pan with foil, and pour into it one cup olive oil. Add the eggplant, and toss in the oil to coat all the pieces. Cover the pan with foil, and bake it in the preheated oven for thirty-five minutes. Remove the eggplant pieces with a slotted spoon, and allow them to drain on paper towel.

Pour the remaining oil into a skillet. Heat and sauté the onions, zucchini, peppers, and garlic in the skillet until the mixture is wilted and lightly colored. Add the tomatoes, tomato paste, parsley, dill, basil, oregano, and black pepper. Simmer ten minutes, stirring occasionally. Add the eggplant and simmer for another ten minutes. Makes twelve servings. (One ¹/₂-cup serving = 50 calories)

FRENCH CARROT SALAD

This salad is not only healthful and delicious, but it gives a lovely splash of color to our table. It is particularly beautiful when served on crisp leaves of Boston lettuce or romaine.

5 large carrots, peeled and trimmed
¹/₂ cup dried currants (raisins may be substituted)
2 tablespoons corn oil
¹/₈ teaspoon freshly ground black pepper
Juice of 1 lemon
Juice of 1 orange
¹/₄ cup chopped fresh mint

Shred carrots into a large bowl. Pour in remaining ingredients over carrots. Toss, cover, and refrigerate until well chilled. Makes six servings. (One serving = 48 calories)

APPLE WALNUT SALAD

4 yellow apples (use either Grimes Golden or Yellow Delicious)
4 red apples (Delicious or Staymen Winesap)
³/₄ cup red wine vinegar
3 scallions or small green onions
4 tablespoons walnut oil
1¹/₂ cups chopped celery
1 cup walnut halves

Core and chop apples, but do not peel. Toss with the wine vinegar. Add remaining ingredients and toss once again. Serve immediately. Makes eight servings. (One serving = 71 calories)

BULGUR (OR CRACKED WHEAT) SALAD

4 cups water
2 cups bulgur
1 cup chopped pecans
4 tablespoons chopped parsley
1 grated orange peel
1 cup dried currants (raisins may be substituted)
1 tablespoon olive oil

Combine water and bulgur in large saucepan. Bring to a boil, reduce heat, cover, and simmer for 35 to 40 minutes. Refrigerate uncovered until chilled throughout. Add remaining ingredients and toss. Serve chilled. Makes eight servings. (One ¹/₂-cup serving =60 calories)

CUCUMBER-MINT SALAD

3 large cucumbers, semipeeled (to leave alternating stripes), halved
    lengthwise, and sliced
¹/₂ cup fresh parsley, chopped
1 grated orange peel
¹/₂ cup fresh mint, chopped
¹/₄ cup olive oil
1 cup red wine vinegar
2 packets artificial sweetener

Mix together in a large bowl the cucumbers, parsley, and orange peel. Whisk together the oil, vinegar, and sweetener. Add to the cucumber mixture. Chill thoroughly for at least four hours. Makes eight servings. (One serving = 23 calories)

GREEN SALAD

I love to find different combinations of salad greens to add variety to our meals. Each has a distinctive flavor that brings its own unique character to our table. I usually serve an herbed vinaigrette sauce over them, with a handful of alfalfa sprouts for added vitamins. (One serving = 20 calories)

Combination No. 1	*Combination No. 2*	*Combination No. 3*
Watercress	Romaine	Spinach
Belgian endive	Watercress	Ruby-red lettuce
Walnut pieces	Chicory	Sliced cucumbers or
Boston lettuce		mushrooms
Baby nasturtium		
leaves		

ASPARAGUS CONSOMMÉ

8 cups chicken stock, clarified
2 cups raw asparagus tops (do not use large bottom portion of
    stalk—only just a little more than the tip)
Fresh dill

Bring chicken stock to a boil and add asparagus. Cook just until asparagus is tender. Garnish with chopped fresh dill. Makes eight servings. (One serving = 70 calories)

CARROT AND ORANGE SOUP

1 cup chopped onions
12 large carrots (1 1/2 to 2 pounds)
4 cups chicken stock
1 cup orange juice
Salt and pepper, to taste
1 teaspoon grated orange peel

In a large saucepan or Dutch oven coated with nonstick vegetable spray, sauté onions over low heat until slightly browned. Add carrots and stock, and bring mixture to a boil. Reduce heat and simmer, covered, until carrots are very tender.

Pour mixture through a strainer, reserving the liquids. Transfer the solids to a blender or food processor along with one cup of the strained liquid, and process until smooth. Return the resulting puree to the saucepan, and add the orange juice. Add remaining reserved liquid—one cup at a time—until soup reaches desired consistency. Season to taste with salt and pepper, and sprinkle with orange peel. Simmer until thoroughly heated, and serve immediately. Makes four to six servings. (One serving = 90 calories)

SURPRISE BREAD

3/4 cup unsweetened pineapple juice
1/2 cup water
2 tablespoons honey
2 tablespoons corn oil
1/2 teaspoon ground ginger
1/2 teaspoon ground cinnamon
1/4 cup uncooked bulgur (cracked wheat cereal, no salt or sugar added)
1 tablespoon dry yeast (or 1 premeasured packet)
2 tablespoons buckwheat flour
1/2 cup plain, low-fat yogurt (at room temperature)
1 teaspoon grated orange peel
4 cups unbleached flour
1/2 teaspoon corn oil margarine (or use nonstick vegetable spray)
2 teaspoons evaporated skim milk

In a saucepan, combine the pineapple juice, water, honey, oil, and spices. Bring to a boil, and pour the mixture over bulgur or cracked wheat in a bowl. Stir and allow to cool until it is just warm to the touch.

In another bowl, combine yeast and buckwheat flour. Pour bulgur mixture over yeast mixture and stir. Beat with a wooden spoon for 1 minute. Cover and let stand 15 minutes.

Stir entire mixture once again, and add yogurt and orange peel. Beat until thoroughly blended.

Reserve ¹/₂ cup of the unbleached flour. Add the remaining flour, ¹/₂ cup at a time, to the mixture in the bowl, beating with a wooden spoon after each addition. When dough becomes difficult to handle with a spoon, scoop mixture onto a lightly floured board (using ¹/₂ cup reserved flour), and knead, using just enough flour to make the dough smooth and elastic. Shape into a ball.

Lightly grease a ten-inch metal pie pan with some of the corn oil margarine, or spray with nonstick vegetable spray. Place dough in the middle of the pan and press down until mixture *almost* touches sides. Grease a long sheet of waxed paper (or, again, spray with nonstick spray), and place sheet over the pan, greased side down. Let entire mixture stand at room temperature until it has doubled in bulk, about 1¹/₂ to 2 hours.

Brush dough lightly with milk, but be careful not to let it drip down the sides of the pan.

Preheat oven to 375°. Bake mixture in center of the oven for forty-five minutes. Remove bread from oven and place on rack for ten minutes. With a blunt knife or spatula, remove the bread from the pan and allow it to cool on the rack for 1¹/₂ hours before slicing. Mixture yields fifteen one-inch wedges, or thirty when cut in half. This dish can serve as a good dessert substitute.

Note: This same mixture can also be made into rolls. Just shape dough into thirty balls and place on cookie sheets which have been greased and lightly sprinkled with cornmeal. Brush with evaporated milk and bake at 375° for twenty to twenty-five minutes. (One serving = 119 calories)

SHRIMP MOUSSE

1 can low-calorie tomato soup
1 pint plain, low-fat yogurt

1 cup mayonnaise
Salt and pepper, to taste
Tabasco sauce, to taste
1³/₄ tablespoons gelatin
1 pound shrimp, diced
1 cup celery, diced
¹/₂ cup water
1 cup onion, diced

Mix soup, yogurt, mayonnaise, salt and pepper, and Tabasco sauce. Stir mixture until smooth. Soften gelatin in ¹/₄ cup cold water; add ¹/₄ cup hot water to dissolve, and add to yogurt mixture. Add remaining ingredients, mix well, and pour into lightly greased fish mold. Use stuffed olives for eyes and serve unmolded with crackers.

This dish is an appetizer but can be used in individual molds as a luncheon entree. (One 3-ounce serving = 190 calories)

DIETER'S DIP (FOR CRUDITÉS)

1 cup plain, low-fat yogurt
¹/₄ cup grated celery, cucumber, or carrot
¹/₄ teaspoon seasoned salt
¹/₄ teaspoon dill weed

Simply mix all ingredients together in a medium-sized bowl, and allow to chill. Serve cold, with raw vegetables cut into bite-sized pieces. (One ¹/₄-cup serving = 40 calories)

GREEN PEPPERCORN MUSTARD DIP

1 cup plain, low-fat yogurt
¹/₄ cup prepared Dijon-style mustard
1 small garlic clove, peeled and chopped
1 teaspoon water-packed green peppercorns, drained, plus a few
    additional peppercorns, to taste

Combine the yogurt, mustard, and garlic in a blender or food processor and puree until smooth. Add the whole green peppercorns to taste. Do not process any further. Refrigerate until time to serve. Makes a delicious dip for crudites. (One ¹/₄-cup serving = 35 calories)

FRUIT PUNCH

2 cans unsweetened pineapple juice
1 can unsweetened orange juice
1 cup lemon juice
1 cup lime juice
5 quarts Diet 7-Up, Diet Sprite, or diet ginger ale
Several sprigs of fresh mint
Strawberries (as garnish)

Place the juices in a punch bowl with ice. Just before serving, add the carbonated beverages. To keep the punch fresh, I usually put half of the juices in the punch bowl, and half in a large reserve bowl. Then I add only half of the soda. As the punch bowl gets low, I add the juices from the reserve bowl and add the rest of the soda. Mint sprigs and fresh strawberries floating on the surface of the punch make it a lovely party drink, just the thing for a warm day. For bridal parties, I often add coconut milk—but this adds to the calories. (One glass = 40 calories)

HOT APPLE CIDER—HOT MULLED CIDER

1 gallon unsweetened apple cider
1 tablespoon whole allspice or any spice mixture you prefer
1 stick cinnamon

Heat cider just to the point of boiling, but be careful not to let it boil. Add spices, and allow it to simmer for at least one hour (until fragrance brings everybody running!). Serves sixteen. (One cup = 150 calories)

BEEF WELLINGTON

1 whole beef tenderloin (filet), or eye round roast
1 pound mushrooms
1/4 cup sherry
2 pastry sheets (frozen, or make your own pie crust mix)
2 egg yolks
4 tablespoons water

Preheat oven to 425°. Trim all fat from filet. Place beef on rack in a roasting pan. Place in oven for twenty-five minutes.

Slice mushrooms and sauté in skillet with nonstick vegetable spray until lightly browned. Add sherry and simmer for five minutes. Remove, and set aside.

Roll out pastry three inches longer than the filet, and wide enough to fold edge completely over the top to encase the meat.

Place filet on pastry two inches in from one long side. Cover filet with mushrooms, and pat in firmly. Bring pastry up and over filet to cover it. Moisten edges, press well to seal. Moisten ends, and fold in firmly to seal. Beat egg yolks with water and brush over pastry. Arrange any scraps of pastry into a decorative design on top. Transfer carefully to a baking sheet (to make it easier, I often transfer pastry to baking sheet before placing filet on it). Bake at 425° for twenty-five to thirty minutes. Makes twelve to fourteen servings. (One serving = 250 calories)

RASPBERRY CHICKEN

2 whole fileted chicken breasts
1/4 cup finely chopped yellow onion
1/2 cup sliced fresh mushrooms
4 tablespoons raspberry vinegar
1/4 cup chicken stock, or canned chicken broth
1/4 cup skim milk
1 tablespoon canned crushed tomatoes
16 fresh raspberries (optional)

Cut each chicken breast in half, and flatten by pressing with palm of hand. In a skillet coated with nonstick vegetable spray, brown chicken on both sides. Remove the chicken from the skillet and reserve.

Add the onions and the mushrooms to the skillet and sauté, covered, over low heat until vegetables are tender (about fifteen minutes). Remove the mushroom mixture and reserve.

Add the vinegar to the skillet, and cook uncovered over moderate heat, stirring occasionally, until the vinegar has been reduced to a syrupy spoonful. Whisk in chicken stock, skim milk, and tomatoes, and simmer for one minute. Return the chicken to the skillet and simmer until tender, basting often. Just before serving, add the mushrooms, and cook for one minute. Place the chicken on a serving platter. Add the raspberries to the sauce and cook for one minute more. Pour over chicken, and serve. Makes four servings. (One serving = 140 calories)

BROILED TOMATO CUPS WITH PETITE POIS

6 whole tomatoes (allow at least one half per person)
2 16-ounce packages fresh frozen baby sweet peas

Cut tomatoes in half; remove seeds and much of the pulp, leaving tomato cups. Put tomato cups on broiling pan, and place under broiler until hot and only slightly cooked (not soft).

Place peas in small amount of water in a saucepan. Bring to a boil, reduce heat, and simmer until peas are thawed and hot. Just before serving, fill tomato cups with peas and place on serving platter. Makes twelve servings. (*Note*: Fresh or frozen spinach may be used instead of peas.) (One serving = 30 calories)

POTATO BALLS

6 Idaho potatoes, peeled and cut into balls with large melon baller
3/4 teaspoon thyme
3/4 teaspoon ground ginger
3/4 teaspoon dried dill
1 teaspoon corn oil margarine
Ground red pepper (cayenne)
Dash paprika

Boil potato balls in just enough water to cover them until almost done—not soft or mushy. Add half of ginger, thyme, and dill to water as potatoes cook.

Preheat oven to 400°. Grease baking pan with margarine. Using a slotted spoon, carefully transfer potato balls to baking pan. Sprinkle potatoes with dashes of red pepper and the remaining thyme, ginger, and dill. Bake at 400° for ten minutes. Stir potatoes gently, and bake for a few minutes more, until balls are browned evenly. Place on serving tray, sprinkle with paprika, and serve. Makes twelve servings. (One potato ball = 40 calories)

GRAPEFRUIT-AVOCADO SALAD

3 grapefruits
1 avocado pear
1 pomegranate
1 head leaf lettuce or Bibb lettuce
2 kiwi fruits (optional)

Peel grapefruit and section. Peel avocado, remove pit, and

slice avocado into strips. Peel half of pomegranate and seed, reserving the seeds. Arrange lettuce on salad plates. Arrange three grapefruit slices and two avocado slices on each plate. Top with Fruit Dip (see recipe included earlier in this section), and sprinkle pomegranate seeds on dip. If you use the kiwi fruit, peel and slice. Arrange a couple of kiwi slices on top of dip, and then scatter seeds. Makes twelve servings. (One serving = 50 calories)

POACHED PEARS IN RED WINE

6 tablespoons lemon juice
12 almost-ripe pears
1 1/4 cups red wine
1 teaspoon ground cinnamon
3 tablespoons honey
1 1/2 cups unsweetened apple juice
1 small cinnamon stick
Cool Whip (optional)
Nutmeg (optional)

Pour lemon juice into a small bowl. Peel pears, leaving stem. Drop each pear into lemon juice, coating it to keep pear from discoloring.

Combine red wine, ground cinnamon, honey, apple juice, and cinnamon stick in large Dutch oven or similar pot. Bring to a boil. Arrange pears in a standing position, and spoon liquid over them. Cover and simmer twenty minutes, or until tender. Transfer pears to serving dish or individual dishes.

Allow remaining liquid to simmer until reduced by one-third. Pour liquid over pears, and refrigerate until it is time to serve. This dish is best when served chilled. Just before serving, top each pear with a spoonful of Cool Whip, and sprinkle with grated nutmeg. Makes twelve servings. (One serving = 40 calories)

CINNAMON-KISSED COFFEE

I serve brewed decaffeinated coffee, but I usually dress it up with a touch of cinnamon. Put one teaspoon of ground cinnamon and one small stick of cinnamon on top of the coffee grounds before brewing. This method works well with either perk or filter-drip models.

BROWN AND WILD RICE

3/4 cup brown rice
1/2 cup wild rice
2 cups water

Place all the ingredients together in a saucepan, and bring to a boil. Stir once with a fork, turn to low, cover, and allow to simmer thirty to forty-five minutes. (One 1/4-cup serving, = 44 calories)

ARTICHOKE BOTTOMS AND PETITE POIS

2 cans artichoke bottoms
3 packages fresh frozen baby sweet peas

Place artichokes in a saucepan and heat. Cook peas according to directions on the package but without adding any salt. With a slotted spoon, remove the artichoke bottoms and place on a serving platter. Fill with cooked peas and serve. Makes twelve servings. (One serving = 40 calories)

MERINGUE ELEGANTE

1 quart strawberries, fresh or thawed frozen
2 kiwi fruits, peeled and sliced
Cool Whip
Meringues

To Make Meringues:
5 egg whites, at room temperature
1/4 teaspoon cream of tartar
3/4 cup sugar
1 teaspoon almond extract

Line two cake pans with foil, or use spring-form cake pans.

In a small bowl, use a mixer at high speed to beat the egg whites and cream of tartar until it forms soft peaks. Beat in sugar, one tablespoon at a time, until dissolved. Beat in almond extract. Mixture should now stand in stiff, glossy peaks. Preheat oven to 275°. Spread meringue mixture 1/2-inch high in each pan. Bake at least one hour, or until golden brown. Cool for 10 minutes. Remove from foil and cool on a rack.

Just before serving, place one meringue on a serving platter. Cover meringue with Cool Whip topping, place strawberries on topping, and cover with the second meringue. Cover top of second meringue with Cool Whip, and arrange kiwi slices on it. Makes twelve servings. ($^{1}/_{2}$ of one serving $=$ 134 calories)

WILD RICE CASSEROLE (An Entree)

1 onion, diced
1 $^{1}/_{2}$ pounds of extra lean ground beef
1 cup wild rice
2 cups diced celery
2 cans low-calorie mushroom soup
2 cans low-calorie cream of chicken soup
1 can water
$^{1}/_{4}$ pound fresh mushrooms, sliced (or 1 small can)
4 ounces cashew nuts
$^{1}/_{2}$ teaspoon Tabasco sauce
1 pimento, chopped
$^{1}/_{4}$ green pepper, chopped (optional)
$^{1}/_{2}$ can evaporated skim milk

In a large skillet, sauté onion until wilted; add ground beef and cook until browned. Using a slotted spoon, transfer onion and beef to casserole dish, combine with remaining ingredients, and bake for 2 hours at 350°. (One serving $=$ 150 calories)

RED, WHITE, AND BLUE DESSERT

1 tablespoon gelatin
$^{1}/_{4}$ cup cold water
1 cup hot water
$^{1}/_{4}$ cup lemon juice
$^{1}/_{4}$ cup sugar substitute
3 egg whites (save yolks for custard mixture below)
$^{1}/_{2}$ cup fresh blueberries
$^{1}/_{2}$ cup fresh strawberries, sliced
(Canned crushed pineapple, drained, or 3 mashed bananas may be substituted for blueberries and strawberries.)

Soak gelatin in cold water to soften. Dissolve in hot water. Add sugar substitute and lemon juice. Chill until mixture falls in sheets from a spoon. Beat the egg whites until stiff. Beat the gelatin mixture into the eggs, and continue beating until mixture begins to thicken. Pour into mold. Add berries at various layers. I like to use a circle mold and put alternating stripes of strawberries and blueberries around it. The berries sink and create an interesting appearance when served with Custard Sauce (see below). Makes six servings. (One $1/2$-cup serving = 40 calories)

Custard Sauce
$1/4$ cup sugar substitute
$1/2$ cup powdered skim milk
2 cups fresh skim milk
4 egg yolks
1 teaspoon vanilla

Combine sugar substitute and powdered milk in saucepan. Add $1/2$ cup skim milk and egg yolks, and heat until smooth. Separately, heat $1 1/2$ cups skim milk. Add to egg mixture. Cook over moderate heat, stirring constantly until temperature reaches 175° (about four minutes). Remove from heat and chill. Add vanilla before serving.

CHILI WITH BEANS

1 pound extra lean ground beef
2 medium onions, chopped
2 cups chopped celery and celery tops
2 pounds soybeans, cooked and ground
$1 1/2$ teaspoons chili powder
$1/2$ teaspoon crushed red pepper (cayenne)
2 teaspoons curry powder
2 small cans tomato paste
6 small cans tomato sauce
1 pound kidney beans, cooked, or 2 cans kidney beans

Brown ground beef in heavy Dutch oven. Add the onion, celery, ground soybeans, and spices. Stir constantly until vegetables are wilted, and add all tomato ingredients. Simmer for several hours, stirring occasionally. Add kidney beans during last half hour of cooking. Makes ten servings. (Crock pot tip: Brown meat, soybeans, onions, and celery first. Then add all ingredients to crock pot and bring to a boil. Turn to low and simmer for several hours.) (One l-cup serving = 175 calories)

BAKED APPLES

10 apples, cored but not peeled
Dash ground cinnamon
Dash ground nutmeg
Dash ground ginger
Dash ground mace
Diet cola (such as Tab, Diet Coke, or RC 100)

Place apples in baking dish. Put a dash of each spice on cored part of apple. Pour diet drink over apples, and bake at 350° for 30 minutes, basting several times. Makes ten servings. (One serving = 94 calories)

SKEWERED LAMB

4 pounds lean lamb, cut into cubes
3 eggplants, peeled and cut into cubes
32 small, whole white onions, peeled
32 cherry tomatoes
2 medium sweet red peppers cut in 1-inch pieces
Fresh mushrooms (optional)

Using marinade recipe below, marinate lamb, eggplant, onions, tomatoes, and sweet pepper for at least one hour at room temperature allowing the liquid to cover the mixture completely. If you wish to include mushrooms, allow them to soak in the marinade for just the last thirty minutes. Drain marinade and reserve.

Alternate vegetables and meat on skewers, and place on rack under preheated broiler. Broil skewers for five minutes, turn, brush with reserved marinade, and broil for three more minutes. Do this twice more, broiling for three minutes on each side and basting with marinade. Meat should be medium rare at this stage, so adjust cooking time to your preferences. Makes sixteen servings. (One 3-ounce serving = 199 calories)

Marinade
$1/2$ cup red wine vinegar
6 teaspoons corn oil
2 garlic cloves, chopped
6 tablespoons pineapple juice (unsweetened)
1 teaspoon ground ginger

1 teaspoon curry powder
1 teaspoon coriander seeds
$^1/_2$ teaspoon red pepper
$^1/_2$ cup cider vinegar
6 teaspoons olive oil
3 tablespoons lime juice
6 tablespoons chicken stock
1$^1/_2$ teaspoons dried basil
3 tablespoons minced fresh parsley

SWEDISH MEATBALLS (An Appetizer)

4$^1/_2$ teaspoons corn oil
2 cloves garlic, minced
$^1/_4$ inch fresh ginger, peeled and minced
1 tablespoon minced celery
2 tablespoons minced sweet red pepper
3/4 teaspoon dried rosemary leaves, crushed
1 tablespoon tarragon vinegar
1 pound extra lean ground beef (or $^1/_2$ pound veal and $^1/_2$ pound
    beef)
3 tablespoons whole wheat bread crumbs
8 dashes ground red pepper (cayenne)
5 tablespoons unsweetened pineapple juice
2 teaspoons minced fresh parsley
$^1/_3$ cup chicken stock
2 whole cloves
1 large green apple, peeled, cored, and sliced

In a skillet, heat half of oil. Add garlic, ginger, celery, and sweet red pepper until lightly browned. Sprinkle mixture with rosemary, add tarragon vinegar, and cook for thirty seconds.

In a large bowl, combine meat and bread crumbs, and pour mixture from skillet over meat. Add red pepper, three tablespoons of pineapple juice, and parsley. Mix together all these ingredients and shape meat into balls.

Heat the remaining oil in skillet, and sauté meatballs until they are lightly browned on all sides. Pour off excess fat. Add chicken stock, remaining two tablespoons pineapple juice, cloves, and apple slices. Bring entire mixture to a simmer. Cover, and cook for twenty minutes, turning meatballs at least twice. (If you prefer, for this last step, the meatballs can be placed in a baking dish and cooked in a 325° oven.) (One 3-ounce serving = 318 calories)

SPANISH CREAM

1 tablespoon plain gelatin
3 cups skim milk
⅓ cup sugar substitute
3 eggs, separated
1 teaspoon vanilla, or ¼ teaspoon almond extract

Soak gelatin in milk for five minutes in the top of a double boiler. Add two tablespoons of the sugar substitute, and cook over boiling water until dissolved. Beat into the egg yolks two tablespoons of the sugar substitute, and add to the dissolved gelatin mixture.

Cook over hot (not boiling) water until mixture coats spoon. Chill until mixture is thick and syrupy. Add vanilla and fold in stiffly beaten egg whites with remaining sugar substitute. Turn into a mold, and chill until set.

Chocolate, caramel, and fruit sauces may be used as a topping, though they add significantly to the calories. (One serving = 76 calories)

LEMON CHICKEN

1 broiling chicken, cut up, skinned, with wing tips removed
1½ teaspoons minced fresh parsley
Lemon marinade (recipe below)
1½ teaspoons minced fresh dill

Wash and dry chicken. Place in bowl and pour marinade mixture over chicken, turning to coat completely. Cover bowl tightly and refrigerate for six hours or overnight. Drain chicken, reserving marinade. Preheat broiler and place chicken on broiler pan under broiler for seven minutes. Turn, baste with marinade, and broil for seven minutes. Repeat three times for a total cooking time of thirty-five minutes. Makes four servings. (One 3-ounce serving = 160 calories)

Lemon Marinade
1 teaspoon peeled and minced fresh ginger
4 cloves garlic, minced

2 tablespoons dry sherry
1 tablespoon corn oil
1 teaspoon chili powder
2 shallots, minced
1/4 teaspoon lemon juice
1 tablespoon honey
4 dashes red cayenne pepper
1 teaspoon fennel seed, crushed

Place all ingredients in a mixing bowl, and whisk thoroughly.

HOT SPICED FRUIT

When using canned fruit, choose only "light" variety, that is, fruit that is canned in its own juices with no added sugar.

1 can pineapple chunks
1 can peach slices
1 can pear slices
1 can plums
1 can green grapes
2 cups frozen apple slices (see recipe below)
1 tablespoon allspice
Cool Whip (optional)
Nutmeg (optional)

Drain all fruit, reserving the liquid. Place one half of the juices in a saucepan with one stick cinnamon and one tablespoon allspice or spice mix of your own choosing. Bring to a boil, reduce heat, and simmer for one hour. Ten minutes before serving, add fruit to syrup, heat to boiling, and serve. Fruit may be topped with Cool Whip and a dash of nutmeg. (One 1/2-cup serving = 61 calories)

FROZEN APPLE SLICES OR APPLESAUCE

Fresh apples
1 tablespoon lemon juice

Peel and core apples. Slice and put in a saucepan with the lemon juice. Add water to cover. Bring to a boil, reduce heat, and simmer until tender. Remove apples with a slotted spoon, and place in a freezer container. Freeze overnight.

Frozen Applesauce

Prepare the same way as for sliced apples above. Just simmer longer, until apples are tender and mushy throughout. Drain apples, stir to desired consistency, and pour into container and freeze.

Waffle Topping

To use applesauce mixture as a waffle topping, I reheat the mixture and add ¹/₂ teaspoon cinnamon and ¹/₄ teaspoon nutmeg to each pint of applesauce.

We like frozen applesauce as a snack or as dessert. (One ¹/₂-cup serving = 50 calories)

LOVE WAFFLES

1 cup unbleached flour (or ³/₄ cup flour and ¹/₄ cup wheat germ)
1 cup soybeans, soaked and cooked, then either ground or
   blended
2 teaspoons baking powder, combination type
1¹/₂ cups skim milk
¹/₂ teaspoon salt
1 tablespoon sugar
3 eggs, separated, with yolks beaten and egg whites reserved
5 tablespoons salad oil or melted margarine

Heat the waffle iron. The iron is ready when a drop of water forms a small ball. If the water sizzles, the iron is too hot.

Mix all ingredients together (except egg whites) with a few swift strokes, just as you would with muffin batter. Beat the three reserved egg whites until stiff, but not dry. Fold the egg whites into the batter until they are barely blended.

These waffles are delicious when served with maple syrup, orange syrup, strawberry preserves, or fresh fruit.

If you have sour milk or sour cream, use two eggs instead of three, and then add 1¹/₂ teaspoons baking powder and ¹/₄ teaspoon baking soda. Makes six waffles. (One serving of 2 waffles = 180 calories)

FLOWERING BROCCOLI

1 medium head cauliflower
1 medium bunch broccoli (about 2 pounds)

2 tablespoons lime juice
1/4 cup chopped pecans

Trim cauliflower and cook in a small amount of boiling water until tender, about fifteen minutes. Trim broccoli by using mostly the flowerettes. Split any thick ends, and discard the tough part of the stems. Cook in the same fashion as the cauliflower. To serve, place cauliflower in center of a platter, and arrange broccoli flowerettes all around it. Pour lime juice mixed with pecans over the vegetables. (One 1/2-cup serving = 47 calories)

DIETERS' PARTY MENUS

As I promised, here are some of my favorite combinations of low-calorie dishes that we use to form the centerpiece of delicious party meals. Elegant entertaining begins with a cautious concern about our guests' desire for nonfattening foods. These special menus feature the recipes from the preceding section.

OPEN HOUSE

Crudités
Dip for Dieters (for crudités)
Green Peppercorn Mustard Dip (for crudités)
Fruit Plate (strawberries, pineapple
strips, apples, pears)
Shrimp Mousse
Swedish Meatballs
Fruit Dip
Fruit Punch or Hot Apple Cider
Cheese ball or ham biscuits (for nondieters)

Note: Crudités include raw fresh strips of
zucchini, cucumber, carrots, celery, as well as
radishes, cauliflower, broccoli arranged colorfully
and attractively in bite-sized pieces.

DINNER PARTY No. 1 (Sit Down)

Asparagus Consommé
Beef Wellington
Broiled Tomato Cups, filled with Petite Pois
or chopped spinach
Potato Balls
Grapefruit-Avocado Salad with pomegranate seeds,
and Fruit Dip
Poached Pears in Red Wine
Coffee or Tea

DINNER PARTY No. 2 (Sit Down or Buffet)

Raspberry Chicken
Brown and Wild Rice
Artichoke Bottoms with Petite Pois
Green Salad
Meringue Elegante
Coffee or tea

DINNER PARTY No. 3 (Buffet)

Wild Rice Casserole
Ratatouille
French Carrot Salad
Red, White, and Blue Dessert
Coffee or tea

DINNER PARTY No. 4

Lemon Chicken
Brown and Wild Rice
Flowering Broccoli
Apple Walnut Salad
Hot Spiced Fruit
Coffee or tea

INFORMAL SUPPER

Chili
Corn bread or muffins
Bulgur Salad
Baked Apples
Coffee or tea

BARBECUE SUPPER

Skewered Lamb
Corn on the cob, roasted or boiled
Cucumber-Mint Salad
Spanish Cream
Coffee or tea

BRUNCH MENU No. 1

I particularly love to entertain in the late morning. I feel fresh, and everyone else is fresh too. Best of all, I can relax for the rest of the day!

Tomato Ice
Love Waffles or Pancakes
(toppings include: Hot Cinnamon Applesauce,
fresh or frozen blueberries, Vermont maple syrup,
or low-calorie maple syrup)
Canadian bacon, pork sausage, kielbasa
Coffee or tea

BRUNCH MENU No. 2

Minted Fresh Fruit
Omelet with Assorted Toppings
(toppings include Hot Cinnamon Apples,
watercress, Ratatouille, mushrooms,
and cheddar cheese)
Surprise Bread
Coffee or tea

CHAPTER SIX The Future You

B y now, you've been on the New You diet for seventy days, and you've lost twenty, thirty, or more pounds. You've also firmed up flabby muscles, and you have a new spring to your step, a new color in your cheeks, and a firmer new tone to your body. You are learning things and seeing changes in yourself for the better.

The adventure, however, has just begun! Reaching the end of the ten-week program does not mean your commitment to weight control and your desire to draw on God's resources for daily living have come to an end. Rather, now that you're feeling better, looking better, and growing in all areas of life, you should want to continue in the things that have made all this possible.

You have learned the value of aerobic exercise, and you know some calisthenics that will keep your muscles firm. Stay with them! You have learned new and better eating habits. You also know that lifelong weight control doesn't have to mean drab, monotonous foods or salads twice every day. Good food and lots of variety are available. Stay with them! You have seen that prayer, Bible reading, and application of spiritual principles can give you the motivation and self-discipline you need to make it all work. Stay with them!

The New You you were meant to be is well worth it.

Remember, too, that the primary motivation for weight control is that the bodies we have were made to serve and be the home of our great God. We want to be as fit as we can so that we can serve Him as effectively as possible. We want to show that we care about His temple—that because it is so valuable to Him, it is worth keeping in good shape.

Look to the future expectantly. As you have gone through the seventy days of *The New You* diet, you have opened yourself up to

God in ways you may never have before. In response, He is clearly working in your life for the better. Progress may be slower in some areas than in others, but at the very least you've gained the confidence that just as He has already helped you grow in other areas, so He will also continue to work in these more troublesome spots.

What's more, you've grasped the vision of what the New You can mean, and weight control is just the start. There's a whole New You spiritually, emotionally, and every other way that God is eager to create. You can now begin to understand how that's possible.

As you have lost weight and grown in Him, you have also discovered the truth of that wonderful verse with which we began Day One:

> But those who wait on the LORD
> Shall renew their strength;
> They shall mount up with wings like eagles,
> They shall run and not be weary,
> They shall walk and not faint.

God is good. God is able. And He's not finished with you yet! By His grace, the Future You will have an even more magnificent and abundant life than the New You is now enjoying.